MILES OF FAITH

A Journey from Broken to Bold Service

KRYSTAL HAMMER

MILES OF FAITH

A Journey from Broken to Bold Service

KRYSTAL HAMMER

Published by
CCE PUBLISHING
Edgewater, Florida

Cover image: Used under license from Wararat #829360907
Cover & book design: Cindy Casey/ CCE Publishing

Published by
CCE PUBLISHING
Edgewater, Florida

Printed in the United States of America

Paperback ISBN: 979-8-9929063-0-1
Library of Congress Control Number: 2025906014

Dedication

To my beloved husband, Joe.

Life with you is the greatest road trip – an adventure led by God's hand, filled with winding roads, unexpected detours, and breathtaking moments of His grace.

Through every mile, you have been my steady co-pilot, loving me with the patience and kindness of Christ. You've held the map when I felt lost, prayed with me when the road was uncertain, and reminded me to trust the One who goes before us.

Thank you for loving me as Christ loves the Church, for standing beside me through every twist and turn, and for making this journey a testimony of God's faithfulness.

This book, like our life together, is a gift from Him, and I am beyond blessed to share the road with you.

Table of Contents

Introduction

If you've picked up this book, then I'm glad we're about to take this journey together. Trust me, I'm not claiming to have all the answers – I'm still figuring this out just like you. But here's what I know for sure: the destination is worth the ride.

This journey we're on is messy. It's full of twists and turns, unexpected bumps, and some pretty serious detours. We'll drive through the desert and climb mountains, face both crushing lows and exhilarating highs. But here's the thing – you're not in this alone.

Think of this book as the road trip you didn't know you needed. We're heading toward something amazing – heaven – more beautiful and breathtaking than we can even begin to imagine.

And that hope? It's everything. Thank God for that hope.

But here's the kicker: even though we know where we're headed, that doesn't mean the ride's going to be easy. The road is going to get rough. There will be moments when you want to throw in the towel, moments when you question if it's worth it. But keep going.

This book was written with ministry leadership in mind, but honestly, it's for anyone who's on this crazy ride of the Christian life.

Whether you lead others or just walk alongside them, we all face struggles. And no one should do it alone.

One of the biggest issues in Christianity is loneliness. It's a silent killer. The kind of isolation that eats away at your soul and makes you doubt everything. We'll talk about that, because it's real, and it matters.

I'm writing this book because it's the book I wish I had when I was convinced I was a failure, or worse, a fugitive – two of the most soul-crushing feelings you can experience.

If you've ever felt like you're not good enough, or you're running from something, then you know exactly what I'm talking about.

The temptation to let those feelings take you out is real. But thank God, He's the one who can take you from feeling like you're at the end of your rope to showing you that He's been there all along, waiting to bring you back into the light.

So, what do you say? Will you join me on this journey to something better? To better ministry, a better life, and – most importantly – a closer walk with Jesus? It won't be easy, but I promise it'll be worth it.

Let's go.

Reading this Book

The first portion of each chapter is the story of our trip, while the second portion is an interpretation of it, and how it applies to our lives. Each chapter pertains to different seasons and how they affect not only us, but those around us.

It's amazing to see the different seasons that God takes us through. Not everyone will go through every season, but we should all learn how to handle each season.

Let's begin the journey!

At Least You're on the Road

It can start with a picture
Or when you find a note.
It can start with a broken heart
When you're feeling all alone.

The memories come flooding back
Stronger than you thought they could.
And before you know you're lookin' back
A little more than you should.

It's okay to look in the rearview mirror
But I don't want you to crash
It's easy to swerve into the other lane
When all you look at is the past.

The road is narrow and the lanes are thin.
Sometimes we don't like the landscape we're in.
At least we have One that lightens the load –
At least we're on the road.

His yoke is easy, His burdens are light
But only when we ride in the passenger side.
We may not know what's around the bend,
At least we know where the path will end.

And though we try to pick up our slack
And make up for all of the things that we lack,
He loves us so and we tend to forget.
We keep looking back more than we care to admit.

It's okay to look in the rearview mirror
But I don't want you to crash
It's easy to swerve into the other lane
When all you look at is the past.

Times and trials, toils and fears
There's only one way to make it through our years.
Don't look back, keep lookin' at Him.
Don't focus on the landscape you're in.
Keep in your mind where this road ends.

The road is narrow and the lanes are thin.
Sometimes we don't like the landscape we're in.
At least we have One that lightens the load –
At least we're on the road.

– Krystal Hammer

Part I

Chapter 1

Here We Go!

✞

"Honey, are you ready yet? Everyone's already in the car!" Angie called from the driveway, her voice tinged with impatience.

"Yes, just grabbing this last bag – be right there!" Kyle shouted back, tossing the bag into the van with one hand as he fumbled for the keys with the other.

If he was honest, Kyle wasn't sure he was ready at all. He knew, deep down, that this trip was something he and his family needed to take.

His dad had made it clear in his will – he wanted Kyle's family to move into the homestead. The house, the life, everything had to change. The inheritance – a beautiful piece of land on the other side of the country – was too big to ignore.

When they saw the property, Kyle and Angie knew immediately: this was it. True to form, his dad had known exactly what they needed, even if they hadn't been ready for it. It was a big leap, but one they felt they had to take.

They had sold what they could, given away or discarded the rest, and now, here they were, packed up and ready to go. But the weight of it all was starting to settle in.

"Dad, is this really what you want for me? To just drop everything? Uproot our whole life and start over?" Kyle thought to himself, anxiety creeping in. "It's so... uncomfortable."

The thought lingered for a moment, but he knew the answer. Yes. That quiet voice inside reminded him: this was the right choice.

And just like that, the nervousness started to fade.

Taking a deep breath, he glanced back at the house one last time. The sold sign still staked firmly in the front yard – a symbol of the life they were leaving behind.

"Alright, let's do this."

He gave Angie a reassuring smile, climbed into the driver's seat, and turned the key. Their two boys, Joshua (named after Kyle's dad) and Jacob, were already buckled in, happily munching on snacks and chatting away.

Kyle put the van in reverse, ready to hit the road. Then his eyes flicked down to the gas gauge – a quarter tank.

"Hey, Angie, do we have any gas coupons? I've only got a quarter tank," Kyle said, trying to keep his voice steady.

Angie started digging through her purse, then looked up with a smile. "I actually set aside some cash for gas from the house sale. We'll be fine! We should stop at the station on Madison, though – it has the best prices."

Relief washed over Kyle. They had barely scraped by with the house sale, and every penny counted. "Madison it is, then," he agreed, backing out of their driveway for the last time.

"This is going to be good for us. It's going to be great for our family," he thought as he put the van in drive and headed toward Madison. They had enough cash for gas, the kids were in good spirits, and the road ahead seemed wide open.

"Dad knew what he was doing." Kyle thought, reminding himself with certainty. "I was crazy to doubt this. Sure, there will be bumps in the road, but I can handle it. We'll handle it."

They reached the Madison station, and as he pumped the gas, the anxiety that was clouding his thoughts lifted. The low gas prices and the extra cash in their pocket made the whole thing feel ... almost euphoric.

He found himself grinning, his fingers tapping along the side of the van as the gas meter climbed.

After Angie took the kids inside to use the restroom one last time, Kyle topped off the tank. He wasn't about to leave one drop behind.

As the van roared to life, the family was ready to hit the open road and Kyle's excitement grew. This was just the beginning. They were off, and the future stretched out before them, full of promise.

~ ~ ~ ~ ~

Much like what Kyle faced when deciding to embark on his journey, answering the call to follow Jesus can feel overwhelming. Even with the reassurance we receive, doubt often creeps in, fueled by the fear of the unknown. The questions can feel relentless, like a storm cloud hanging over us:

1. *Will God actually take care of me?*
2. *Where will God send me?*
3. *What if He asks me to do something I don't want to do?*
4. *Does this mean I have to give up things I hold dear?*

I can speak to these concerns from experience, and here's what I've learned:

1. **God will always provide.** Even when it looks uncertain or "sketchy," God has a way of showing up just when we need Him. I've seen it happen too many times in my own life to believe anything else.

2. **God will send you exactly where you need to go.** It might not always make sense at the time, but trust me, His plan is always the best one.

3. **Yes, God will ask you to do things you don't want to do.** But here's the catch: those very things will be the most important, the most reward-

ing, and the most transformative for you. He will bless you in ways you can't even imagine when you step into the discomfort.

4. **Sometimes, yes, we do have to give up the things we hold most dear.** But in the process, we learn that the treasures of this world pale in comparison to the treasures awaiting us in heaven (Matthew 6:19-21).

At the start of our journey of following Jesus wherever He takes us, these questions can seem daunting. But as we learn to trust, something shifts inside us. We go from feeling overwhelmed to being excited about the incredible privilege of serving God. What a joy it is to know that He is leading us on a journey of purpose, adventure, and growth!

Think about Kyle: one of the first steps he took was to fill up his tank. Before setting out on any long journey – especially one as monumental as ministry – it's crucial to make sure we're prepared. Just as Kyle needed to top off his gas tank, we, too, need to seek wisdom and guidance from those we trust. This might mean gathering resources, reaching out to mentors, or simply taking time to prepare spiritually and emotionally.

So, I ask you: *Have you filled up your tank today?* Are you ready for the journey ahead, knowing that God will provide, guide, and equip you every step of the way?

Chapter 2

Dry Roads

✝

As they drove through town, Kyle and Angie sat in a quiet, reflective silence, each lost in their own thoughts. The familiar sights – the streets, the shops, the landmarks – flashed by, each one holding a memory, a moment from their past.

Occasionally, one of them would break the silence with a quiet, nostalgic remark: "Remember when we …?" or "I haven't thought about that in years …"

It was as if time both stretched on endlessly and moved too quickly all at once. They were leaving so much behind – so many memories, so much history – and yet, the future ahead felt like a blank page waiting to be written.

Moving across the country wasn't a decision they'd taken lightly. It was a monumental change. But they had made their choice, and now they were stepping forward into the unknown, hand in hand.

Kyle trusted his father's wisdom. In his letter to Kyle, his dad had insisted that this move – though daunting – would ultimately be better for their family. And Angie, without hesitation, trusted Kyle. Together, they were stepping into the future, but not without a deep sense of what they were leaving behind.

"Kyle, do you remember that burger place on the corner?" Angie asked, squeezing his hand as they passed the spot. "That's where you and I first met!"

Kyle chuckled. "How could I forget? My buddy Chris dared me to squeeze ketchup all over the table before we left. I was such an idiot – ended up spraying it all over you instead."

Angie laughed, her eyes lighting up with fondness. "Yeah, young and dumb," she said, teasing, but with a warmth in her voice. "But still so lovable."

Kyle shook his head, a hint of self-mockery in his tone. "I can't believe I did that. I was so thoughtless. Think about the poor server ..." He winced at the memory.

"But hey," Angie said, squeezing his hand tighter, "you and I connected because of that moment. You felt so bad, you drove me home. We ended up talking the whole way, and I thought I was just out for a fun night with friends! Instead, I met the best guy I know."

Kyle grinned, his chest warming at her words.

"I don't know about the best guy," he said, his voice soft with a mixture of humility and pride. He still couldn't quite believe Angie had stuck by him, that she was now willing to leave everything behind to follow him across the country. He was so lucky. "But I guess I'll do."

Angie smiled at him, the kind of smile that made everything else fade into the background.

"We've got so many memories here," she said quietly, her voice laced with a touch of sadness. "Now everything is going to change, huh?"

Before Kyle could answer, a small voice piped up from the backseat.

"Mom, how long until we get there?"

Joshua groaned in his typical big brother fashion.

"Jacob, it's going to be sooooo long. Just eat your goldfish."

"But... what if we don't make it?" Jacob pressed, his voice rising with concern. "What if we get stuck in the car forever? What if we don't like it there?"

Kyle chuckled at his son's overactive imagination, turning his head slightly to meet Angie's gaze.

"We're not going to be stuck in the car forever, buddy. It might feel like forever, but trust me, it won't be," he said, trying to reassure him. Then, in a more serious tone, he added, "And as for the new place – trust me on that one, too, we're going to love it. Grandpa left us that house for a reason. He knew what we needed. There's plenty of space to run and lots of kids in town to play with. You're going to have a blast."

Angie smiled at him, her eyes full of affection and quiet support. Kyle glanced back at her as they made the turn onto the boulevard leading to the interstate.

This was it. They were leaving behind one life, one world, to step into something new, something unknown. But it felt right. It felt like it was meant to be.

"We're all going to love it," he said, more to reassure himself than anyone else. "I'm sure of it."

Angie grinned back at him, her eyes sparkling with a mix of excitement and anticipation.

"I'm sure we will, too," she said, her voice full of warmth. "I just wish we were already there."

Kyle gave her hand a gentle squeeze as the van picked up speed, their past slowly fading into the rearview mirror, and the road ahead stretching out before them. Whatever was waiting for them in Maine, they were ready. They had each other. And they had faith that the best was yet to come.

~ ~ ~ ~ ~

When we begin the journey God has called us to, reality starts to set in. We begin to ask ourselves: *Is God really asking me to leave everything behind and step into the unknown?*

It's easy to look back and long for the comfort of the past, to tell ourselves things were better before we answered His call. But we can't let those fleeting feelings of doubt or nostalgia derail us. Even though it might feel safer to dwell on what we've left behind, we must resist that temptation. God's plans for us are far greater than anything we could imagine. The future He's leading us toward holds blessings and growth that surpasses our past – if only we keep moving forward in faith.

"For I know the plans I have for you," declares the Lord, "plans to prosper you and not to harm you, plans to give you hope and a future."

– Jeremiah 29:11

For we are his workmanship, created in Christ Jesus for good works, which God prepared beforehand, that we should walk in them.

– Ephesians 2:10

These verses are familiar to many Christians, but how often do we truly let them sink deep into our hearts? Instead of embracing them fully, we question, we doubt, and we look back.

Think of Lot's wife – God told her not to look back, yet she did and was turned into a pillar of salt. It's a stark reminder that when God calls us to move forward, dwelling on the past can have serious consequences. We too are warned not to cling to what's behind us:

Do not call to mind the former things,
Or consider things of the past.

– Isaiah 43:18

But Jesus said to him, "No one, after putting his hand to the plow and looking back, is fit for the kingdom of God."

– Luke 9:62

There's nothing wrong with reminiscing – it's natural to reflect on the past. But we must be intentional about not getting stuck there.

Dwelling on what's behind us can keep us from stepping into the future. Trust me, I've been there! Instead, shift your focus to the vision God has given you for what lies ahead. His plans are far greater than anything we could leave behind.

Chapter 3

Speed Bumps

Joshua let out an excited squeal and pointed to the left. "Mom, look over there! That looks like so much fun!"

Angie turned and saw a line of bottle rockets soaring into the air. "Wow! That is pretty cool. Maybe when we're done with this trip we can shoot some of our own!"

She turned to Kyle with a concerned look. "Hey, aren't we going a little fast? I think we're in a school zone."

Kyle glanced at the speedometer: 45 miles per hour. He quickly eased off the accelerator, but it was too late – the car jolted upward as the front wheels hit a steep speed bump, and the boys yelped in surprise. Angie gasped beside him.

"Whoops. I should've been paying more attention," Kyle muttered, slowing the car down to the 15 miles per hour posted on the sign. "Guess I got a little too excited there."

Angie looked at him, wide-eyed. "I'm just grateful we didn't get pulled over – or worse," she said, her voice tight.

"Me too!" Jacob chimed in, his tone a mix of relief and nervous laughter.

"Me three!" Joshua added, sounding just as relieved.

Jacob, ever the storyteller, piped up, "One time, I heard a story about a kid getting hit on this road."

"Jacob!" Angie snapped, turning to him. "Don't talk like that!"

"Yeah, but the kid didn't die. He just broke his leg," Jacob continued, as though oblivious to the tension. "I wonder if it's true?"

Kyle shot a glance in the rearview mirror, trying to shake off the uneasy feeling that was creeping in.

"I don't know about that, but I do know one thing – I'm glad there was no one in front of us when I was speeding!"

They drove in silence for a few miles, the road stretching ahead as Kyle merged onto the interstate. His thoughts were racing, too – his pulse still thumping in his chest from the close call. *This is really happening.* He brought his family on this wild cross-country journey, and already, in the first few minutes, he almost messed it up.

"*I've never even gotten a ticket. I could've hurt someone!*" thought Kyle nervously. He gripped the steering wheel tighter, trying to focus.

Beside him, Angie's thoughts mirrored his own. Nervous, excited, and anxious all at once, they were both grappling with the reality of what they were doing. The weight of the unknown felt heavy. *What if they messed it all up? What if the kids didn't adjust? What if …*

There was just too much uncertainty! Trusting that their new life would be everything they hoped for seemed easier said than done. And getting to the other side of this journey? That was only the beginning.

As if on cue, Joshua's voice broke through the tension.

"Mom, I'm really excited to see our new house. I get to meet new friends and go to a new school. It's gonna be awesome!"

Angie smiled, trying to sound more confident than she felt.

"Yes, Joshua. It's going to be an adventure, that's for sure. I bet you'll make tons of new friends."

But inside, she was questioning everything. Joshua had a hard time making friends, always struggling to fit in. Angie's mother had often said that he wasn't everyone's cup of tea. Angie prayed silently as the car picked up speed on the freeway.

"*We've got this.*" Angie reassured herself.

The uncertainty was still there, hovering over them all. But as they drove further away from the life they'd known, something shifted. There was a quiet resolve, a sense that no matter the bumps along the way – literal or figurative – they were in this together.

And that, somehow, was enough to keep moving forward.

~ ~ ~ ~ ~

It's easy to get excited when you start following Jesus. You'll do whatever it takes, and speed down the road to make changes. It can become stressful, overwhelming, and all-consuming. However, if we go too fast it can cause some major issues. During my own time in ministry, I've seen firsthand the results of going too fast.

Some of them are:

1. Burnout – When we push too hard, we quickly reach the point of not being able to push anymore. Then we are no longer fulfilling the call on our lives. It's hard to balance ministry and rest, but necessary to do so. How can you find the balance? Ask a few people around you if they feel you are living a balanced life. Brace yourself: the answer might hurt! Then make changes accordingly.

2. Dismantled family relationships – Burning the candle at both ends sometimes means sacrificing your family on the altar of ministry. This hurts everyone, and is hard to recover from. If you find your familial relationships fractured, it's time to step back and re-evaluate. What needs to change? Schedule family time into your life (This is important even if you aren't struggling with this. In fact, it can prevent this from happening.).

Remember that your family is your ministry too…no matter what it looks like.

3. Distraction from God – When you are having a hard time following, you have a hard time leading (and we all lead someone). This can lead to a distance between you and God. This is a place you never want to be! If you see this happening in your life, retreat and draw close to Him. He is always there to bring you back. If this isn't something you are struggling with, I encourage you to schedule a retreat twice per year to prevent this distraction from occurring.

4. Isolation – Burning the candle at both ends also means that you are unable to build relationships. We are built for relationship, and we have to allow ourselves space for these relationships. One should always have at least one person who is sowing into your life, and one you are pouring into. More than that, it's wise to have a relationship outside of the ministry you are involved in. If you feel lost on where to start, make a list of your relationships, and start those you would like to build. Begin to work on these relationships in a healthy way.

5. Dysfunction – You can fall to temptation much easier when you are tired and overwhelmed. If you see yourself being tempted in ways that you have overcome, or in new ways, examine what the cause is (note that going too fast isn't always the cause for this). Next, lean on the Lord to provide you with wisdom on how to combat this through the Holy Spirit. Temptation will always exist, but sometimes we put ourselves in situations where we are more easily tempted and we need to remove ourselves from those situations.

Incremental change is still change. Remember to give yourself grace as you are adjusting. If you find yourself in any of these places, pray first. While we know this in our heads, we can't forget this in our hearts. I would encourage you to journal about the things you are going through so that you can see the results.

When I first stepped into a vocational ministry role, I threw myself into it wholeheartedly. I was working 50-60 hours per week, and putting my family on the backburner. I did little to care for myself, and I didn't understand that it's okay to take a break. Before long, I became emotional and overwhelmed. I didn't take the steps above because no one showed me how. The end result was a huge step back. At the time, I decided that full-time ministry wasn't for me. I'll talk more about this in Chapter 5.

Fast forward a few years, and God was clear that I was called into full-time ministry, and I was back in the saddle. However, by this time I had learned that I needed to keep myself from burnout, distraction, isolation, and dysfunction.

With these tools in my toolbelt, I embraced my role. I still needed my spouse to help me see when I wasn't keeping space available for my family, but I did much better.

Now, I take time to retreat when I see distance building. I build relationships with mentors and mentor others, and I am intentional with my availability to my family.

While I still struggle at times, I now know what flags to look for, and that can make all of the difference. You too can see this in your life. While it will always be a work in progress, allowing the work to happen can change things greatly.

My hope is that you don't have to go through what I did to experience freedom from pushing too hard.

Chapter 4

Potholes

✠

After the first 100 miles, Kyle turned the family van onto another highway.

"I heard there are some amazing sights along this route, guys," Kyle exclaimed. "There's a giant dinosaur and some cool sculptures!"

Angie shot him a skeptical look. "Kyle, are you sure about this? This trip is already pretty long."

"I'm sure!" Kyle replied with enthusiasm. "The kids will love it! And it only adds an hour."

Just then, the van lurched unexpectedly. "*What was that?*" Kyle thought, glancing at the road. "*I didn't see anything... well, I wasn't paying the best attention.*" He quickly checked the rearview mirror. "*Ah, a pothole! A big one, too. I hope the suspension's okay. I just got it aligned!*"

"Ugh," Angie groaned. "My coffee is everywhere! I can't believe you didn't see that coming," she muttered, starting to clean up the mess.

In the backseat, Jacob began to cry. Kyle glanced at him through the rearview mirror.

"What's wrong, buddy?"

Between sobs, Jacob sniffled, "I spilled my juice on my lap!" His cries grew louder.

Kyle quickly pulled over to the side of the road, his thoughts turning to the consequences of his distraction. *"I know I'm going to hear about this later,"* he thought.

Stepping out of the car, Kyle immediately realized he shouldn't have been thinking that way at all. He should have been more focused. The mess and the tears were his responsibility.

"I'm really sorry, everyone," he said, feeling the weight of the moment. "I should've been paying more attention."

Angie shot him a look that silently conveyed, *Yes, you should have!* But then she softened and said, "It's okay. It's easy to get distracted."

As Angie mopped up the coffee, Kyle helped Jacob change into fresh clothes, as his jeans were soaked through. Throughout the process, Jacob continued excitedly talking about the big dinosaur, oblivious to the mess. At just nine years old, he was already able to move on from the spill without a second thought. Kyle couldn't help but admire his son's ability to let things go so easily, something Kyle himself still struggled with. He stuffed the wet jeans into a plastic bag, settled Jacob back in his seat, and took a moment to look over at Joshua, who was happily absorbed in his toy cars.

"I've got it pretty good," Kyle thought, *"So why is it so easy for me to dwell on the little mistakes?"* He sighed and reminded himself, *"Let it go, Kyle. No one's perfect. Just accept it."*

Kyle had always been a perfectionist, and his desire to get everything right often held him back. But as he pulled back onto the road, he made a decision: from now on, he would focus more on the journey ahead and less on the missteps along the way.

~ ~ ~ ~ ~

Despite our best intentions, it's easy to lose focus on what truly matters and get caught up in the distractions around us. Before we know it, we've made a misstep, and the people around us bear the consequences.

I've experienced this myself on more than one occasion.

One instance stands out. I was working in the nonprofit sector at a Christian organization, feeling pretty good about myself. I had recently lost some weight, I was confident in my abilities at work, and life seemed to be going well. But the nature of my job kept me in the public eye, and I let myself get distracted by the opinions of others – how I looked during presentations, how well I was performing, and what my coworkers thought of me.

And then, it all started to unravel.

My marriage, which had already been carrying some unaddressed issues from the past, hit a breaking point, leading to a heated argument with my husband. My kids started to struggle in school, and my own relationship with God began to weaken.

All of this happened because I had lost sight of what was truly important. I had let the distractions of the world pull me away from the things that mattered most.

Thankfully, it only took a spilled cup of coffee (literally) to snap me back into focus. God intervened before things spiraled too far. I know this isn't always the case, but in this moment, I was able to clean up the mess and get things back on track.

We all make mistakes, though I often struggle to accept that truth. I prefer to do things perfectly the first time.

Do you know who doesn't have trouble with the fact that we mess up? God. He is endlessly patient with us, gently shaping our hearts and guiding us toward the people

He created us to be. The key is allowing Him to do that – by not dwelling on our mistakes, but moving past them and pressing forward toward Him. It's something we may know in our minds but often forget to embrace in our hearts.

God is patient with us, and He can handle our mistakes. So, let's keep moving toward Him.

The Lord is not slow about His promise, as some count slowness, but is patient toward you, not willing for any to perish, but for all to come to repentance.

– 2 Peter 3:9

The only one who is without mistake is God. When we truly understand that He is patient with us, that He knows our humanity better than we do, and that He knew we would make mistakes before we even did, we can begin to grasp the depths of His grace.

God saw our missteps coming from the very beginning, so why do we continue to beat ourselves up over them? When we focus on our flaws and failures, we dishonor God because He sees us as so much more than that.

Despite our mistakes, He loves us unconditionally. God is greater than our failures. Keep your focus on that truth, and He will guide you into places you never imagined. His grace is enough – every single day.

Chapter 5

Cracks in the Road

✞

After awhile, Kyle glanced at the gas gauge. He wanted to make sure to top off the tank before they went through the desert.

"*Made a good choice getting the hybrid,*" he thought. "*At least I can plan where we stop – don't want to just pull over anywhere.*"

He turned to Angie. "Do you know how far the next town is? It'll be good to fill up before we head into the middle of nowhere."

Angie quickly checked her phone. "Looks like it's about 20 miles. Not too far."

"Good. That will be a good time to get gas, stretch our legs, and grab some snacks," Kyle replied.

Angie looked back at the kids. "Makes sense. We could all use a bathroom break."

A few minutes later, Kyle took the exit and started down the road into the small town. But as he drove, he noticed the roads growing rougher – cracks were scattered everywhere, and sidewalks were uneven with weeds poking through. It looked like the place hadn't seen a bit of care in years. It didn't even seem like a very small town.

"There's the gas station, Dad!" Joshua said from the backseat. "Can we go in and get some snacks?"

Kyle pulled up to the station and smiled. "Mom'll take you inside, but wait for her. Don't just run in there."

Joshua rolled his eyes. "I would never do that."

Jacob snickered. "You totally would! Remember the time you ran off at the grocery store while Mom was putting stuff in the car?" He always remembered stuff like that.

"No," Joshua muttered, crossing his arms and frowning.

"It wasn't that long ago!" Jacob exclaimed. "Mom had to run after you, and she was so mad!"

Angie and Kyle tried not to laugh, exchanging amused glances. Kyle smiled at Joshua. "Make sure you wait for Mom, alright?"

With that, Kyle got out of the car to fill up the tank. He could still hear the boys bickering as Angie took them into the station.

Kyle's mind wandered as he pumped gas, his thoughts lingering on the town's neglected sidewalks, the cracked parking lot, and the road ahead that abruptly stopped where it had been repaved.

"How does that even happen?" he wondered. "Did they just forget this part? Maybe they're planning to come back."

It made him think about life. "*Sometimes you forget to maintain something, and before you know it, it's all falling apart. Like my eating. I've totally fallen off track. Now I've got this gut. But hey, grinning wide at least it's a nice gut.*"

Suddenly, Angie grabbed his arm, startling him.

"Sorry, I didn't mean to scare you!" she said, smiling.

"All good," Kyle chuckled. "I was just thinking about my nice dad gut, and how it came to be."

Angie laughed. "It is a nice gut! Speaking of..." She tossed him a bag of sour cream and onion chips as she walked past. "Here you go."

Kyle laughed along with her, but inside, he couldn't help thinking, "*I really need to work on that gut. I'll start eating healthy after this trip.*"

~ ~ ~ ~ ~

Earlier I mentioned the things that can happen when you go too fast in life and forget God. Now I'm going to talk about something that happens all too easily in our lives: neglect. I had a time when I went too fast in my ministry career. When you don't catch yourself, going too fast reaches the next stage: neglect.

My life became defined by exhaustion and frustration. I was always overwhelmed. I was running full-speed ahead – faster if I could – trying to do everything on my own. I had far too much on my plate, and I wasn't relying on the Holy Spirit to refresh and replenish me each day.

Instead, I tried to do it all myself. I remember not being present for my kids, my husband, or my work. I felt empty inside, even though the people around me thought I had it all together. But most of all, I remember feeling sorry for myself.

I'm deeply grateful to a mentor who encouraged me to step back, pray, and assess what I was doing. At first, I ignored that advice, continuing to push forward while neglecting the care of my spiritual life. I avoided maintenance in my relationships and health as well. It took a few more months before I finally made the decision to step back, pray, and re-center myself.

God is so good. Even when we neglect Him, He never forgets us. He is always there, patiently guiding us back when we stray. I'm thankful we don't serve a God who thinks like us, but one who sees our need before we even recognize it.

After I took the time to focus on Him, everything started to fall into place. I became a better parent, a better wife, and I was able to do my job – and minister – more effectively.

I learned a hard lesson: if I don't prioritize my relationship with God, life becomes chaotic.

If we don't take action when we notice these lapses, they can turn into something far more serious.

It's easy to neglect our spiritual health during certain seasons of life. There are a million reasons we do it: sometimes we forget or get distracted; sometimes it's because we know we'll have to confront sin or change things in which we're comfortable. But just like neglecting our physical health, neglecting our spiritual health can have serious consequences.

Physically: If we decide to disregard our health – eating junk food, skipping exercise, or binge-watching on the couch – we pay the price. In ministry, this is especially easy to do. We justify unhealthy habits because we're "doing it for God" – grabbing fast food on the way to a hospital visit, snacking while prepping sermons, relying on caffeine or soda to get us through long hours. But that's no excuse.

Spiritually: The same neglect can happen when we fail to maintain our relationship with God. If we skip prayer or don't allow Scripture to penetrate our hearts, we're ignoring the necessary upkeep of our spiritual well-being. In ministry, it's easy to spend all our time serving others without letting God minister to us. We can get so caught up in the work that we stop listening to what God is saying. Over time, our hearts can harden, and we'll find ourselves distant from God.

If we don't catch these issues early, they lead to discouragement, disappointment, and bitterness. Eventually, we'll crash.

Take it from one who learned the hard way: eat the healthy food, make time to breathe, listen for God's voice, and take care of both your physical and spiritual well-being.

You'll be able to do far more when you prioritize your health now.

Chapter 6

The Mirage

✠

As Kyle merged back onto the road, he stole a glance at his boys in the backseat, his heart swelling with pride. They were playing together with their Legos and dinosaurs, their laughter filling the van. For once, there was peace between them – something Kyle wasn't used to, especially with how much his boys could bicker. Still, there they were, enjoying each other's company for a few precious moments.

His gaze shifted to Angie, who was fluffing her "road trip pillow," as she called it. It had seen better days – her poor pillow was getting squished and beaten – but Kyle knew how important it was for her to get it just right if she was going to be able to sleep.

"And, of course, she's got me to boot," he mused with a chuckle. *"Although, once she starts snoring, I might not be so grateful."*

Angie shot him a sideways glance, sensing his amusement. "What? I need it to be comfy so I can sleep!" she said, her voice filled with mock indignation.

"I know, I know," Kyle replied with a grin, knowing full well she had no idea what was going through his mind.

With a last fond look at Angie, Kyle turned his attention back to the road. For the next few hours, it would be nothing but desert, with miles of endless, arid land stretching out before him. He had never driven this route before, but he had heard that it was a long, tough drive. He settled into his seat, bracing himself for what would surely feel like the longest stretch of his journey.

Before long, Angie and the kids were all asleep, leaving Kyle alone with his thoughts. As he looked ahead, his mind began to drift toward their new home. He'd seen pictures – a charming wraparound porch, a tire swing hanging from a massive oak tree, a playset for the kids. He imagined what it would be like to live there with his family. He pictured himself grilling burgers on the porch while Angie relaxed in a chair, reading a book, and the kids played on the tire swing. It was going to be perfect.

But then, out of the corner of his eye, he saw something that brought him back to full attention. He rubbed his eyes and looked again. It looked like a lake. But that couldn't be right – he didn't remember hearing about any lakes on this route. The road should curve to avoid it, but it didn't seem to.

"*Maybe there's been a flood,*" Kyle thought, staring intently ahead. "*Maybe it's just some water on the road.*"

He slowed down cautiously, but he didn't want to wake anyone up, so he didn't hit the brakes too hard. "*This is strange. I've heard of mirages, but this is something else. This doesn't look like any mirage I've seen on TV,*" Kyle thought.

His curiosity mounted, but he kept driving, trying to make sense of it. He glanced in the rearview mirror – there was a car behind him, and it was gaining on him quickly.

"*That's strange,*" Kyle thought. "*Why aren't they slowing down?*"

To his surprise, the car zoomed past him, a woman at the wheel, glaring at him as she went by. Kyle felt a knot form in his stomach.

"*Doesn't she see the lake ahead?*" he thought anxiously.

But what happened next was even more shocking. The car didn't swerve or slow down; it drove straight into the lake. For a split second, the vehicle seemed to sink, the water almost swallowing it up, and then, just like that, it vanished.

Kyle blinked in disbelief. *"It IS a mirage!"* He slapped his forehead, embarrassed. *"How did I fall for that?"*

"I can't believe I was so stupid. A mirage! I should have seen it coming in this heat. He let out a relieved sigh. At least I'm not driving into a lake. And thank goodness Angie's asleep. She would either think we were really driving into a lake or know exactly what it was and make me feel like a fool."

With a self-deprecating laugh, Kyle pressed the gas pedal, picking up speed and continuing toward their next destination. Angie and the boys slept on, unaware of his brief moment of foolishness. As the miles ticked by, Kyle promised himself he would stay alert from now on – no more getting fooled by desert illusions.

~ ~ ~ ~ ~

Sometimes things don't look quite like you think they will. You find out the hard way that someone has put up a front about who they really are. And before you know it, you've been duped.

As someone who prides herself on being a natural skeptic, it's rare for me to be caught off guard. But in this case, I had failed to pay attention to the details.

I had allowed myself to be distracted by the surface – by the glitz and glamor – without seeing what was beneath it all.

How could this happen when I thought I was paying attention? Let me explain.

A little while ago, I had just embraced full-time ministry at a local church. In this season of change, I was excited to build authentic relationships and trust that God was guiding every step of my journey.

During a retreat with our church leadership – a time meant for fellowship, learning, and spiritual renewal – I found myself among people I deeply respected.

I had grown close to many, believing that we all carefully maintained our boundaries in both word and deed.

But in the quiet of one night, in the midst of what I thought was a safe space, a message arrived from someone I trusted. In that exchange, a proposal was made that challenged the very boundaries I held dear.

The nature of the suggestion, unexpected and entirely out of line with our shared values, left me momentarily stunned. I responded firmly with a clear no.

Looking back, I wish I could say that I immediately went to the church leadership to report the incident. I wish I had done that.

But the me at that time struggled with shame. I thought I must have done something to cause this (in part due to unrealized childhood trauma).

I convinced myself that if I had just been more careful – if I had dressed differently, acted differently, or paid more attention – this never would have happened.

I felt like it was somehow my fault, that I didn't have the right to say anything.

Now, with hindsight, I realize none of this was my fault. But that doesn't mean I shouldn't have taken additional precautions to protect myself from such a situation in the future.

After that experience, I put up stronger guardrails in my life. I started to guard not just against the appearance of sin but against sin itself.

This shift in perspective changed the way I communicated, the way I thought, and the way I behaved.

I became much more vigilant, watching my surroundings and guarding my heart.

Maintaining vigilance is an essential part of ministry. If we aren't careful, we can easily fall into traps laid out for us by the enemy.

The Bible warns us about this:

> Be of sober spirit, be on the alert. Your adversary, the devil, prowls around like a roaring lion, seeking someone to devour.[9][a] So resist him, firm in your faith, knowing that the same experiences of suffering are being accomplished by your[b] brothers and sisters who are in the world.
>
> *– 1 Peter 5:8-9*

I pray you don't have to learn this lesson the hard way like I did. But if you do, remember that God is always ready to guide you back on track. His grace is abundant, and He is always there to restore and protect you.

Chapter 7

Wait! Who's Driving Again?

✝

As they left the desert behind, Kyle finally began to relax behind the wheel. No more mirages. The road ahead curved gently toward the mountains, and he smiled – he loved mountain driving. He glanced in the rearview mirror; the boys were still fast asleep. He looked over at Angie. She was out cold, too.

"I'm so glad they didn't know what was going on in my head," Kyle thought as he drove. *"That would have been embarrassing!"*

His mind wandered back to the mirage and how easily he had been tricked. He made a silent vow to never let something like that happen again. And that woman – she had been so mad at him! It was almost ridiculous. He hadn't known what was going on. He had been trying to stay safe, right? And in a way, wasn't he keeping her safe, too? Except that he wasn't ... because it had all been a mirage. He shook his head at himself.

Glancing at the clock, he realized it was time to stop for the night. He nudged Angie.

"Honey, I think it's time we call it a night. Can you find us a hotel?"

After a few minutes, Angie pulled out her trip planner. "We've got about 50 miles to go until we get to the one I reserved." She shot him a playful glare.

Kyle smirked. Of course she had it all planned out. "Hey, you never told me about that! We could have driven right past the hotel!"

After another hour on the road, they arrived at the hotel, settled in, and snuggled together for a movie. Before long, they were all fast asleep.

The next morning, Kyle was eager to hit the road again. They grabbed a quick breakfast and were off. A couple of hours later, the road began to climb, and the landscape shifted – first scrubby brush, then small trees, and finally large, towering trees – both deciduous and coniferous.

"*This is perfect,*" he thought. "*I'm glad we took this route. The other way was all flat ... no thanks. I don't care if it's slower, this is the way to go.*"

As he rounded the next curve, he found himself behind a logging truck just turning onto the road. He slowed down, waiting for the truck to finish its turn. But then, the truck began crawling along at a glacial pace. Kyle felt his frustration bubbling up.

"*This guy!*" he thought. "*Why couldn't he have just waited to turn? Why ruin my drive? Everything was going so well, and now this! I'll never get another chance to drive this road again – why me?*"

He stewed in his frustration, until he felt Angie's hand on his thigh.

"Are you okay?" she asked, her voice light but concerned. "You're mumbling and grunting over there. Sounds like you're on the struggle bus."

Kyle shot her a look, and her grin vanished instantly. He turned his gaze back to the road, tightening his grip on the wheel.

"Did you know you were grunting?" she asked again, glancing out the windshield. "I get it, the truck's ruining your drive. But we could pull over and let him go for a bit. There's a pull-out right there."

But Kyle, irritated, passed it by.

"If we pull over, we'll just catch up to him again," he muttered. "I'll pass him when I can. I just need to keep going." He let out a dramatic sigh.

Angie didn't press him. She knew better than to try to fix it in that moment. Instead, she opened her book and let him vent in peace. The kids were still asleep, and she decided to enjoy the rare quiet time.

After what felt like forever, Kyle was finally able to pass the truck. Thankfully, the trucker saw him and pulled aside. Kyle zoomed by in a rush of irritation, and Angie shook her head.

"He'll calm down eventually," she thought. *"He just needs to go with the flow. But, right now? He's not ready to hear it."*

It took about 30 minutes, but Kyle finally started to relax. Then, he realized just how ridiculous his frustration had been.

"That driver didn't control his route." Kyle thought sheepishly. *"He didn't intend to inconvenience me. Grunting and muttering ... I feel like such a fool. Poor Angie didn't deserve to bear the brunt of my frustration."* He glanced over at her.

"I'm sorry I got so mad. It was dumb."

"It wasn't dumb. Okay, maybe a little," Angie teased with a smile. Then she grew more serious. "But I get it. You good now?"

"Yeah," Kyle said, sheepishly. "I can't believe I did that."

"We all have our moments," Angie replied. "I've been there too. But next time? If you're so upset that it happened, be ready for it. Expect the trucker to turn onto the road. If one doesn't, you're good. If one does, you'll be prepared."

Kyle chuckled. "Angie, that's deep."

"Well ..." she said with a grin, "I have my moments." They both laughed, and the tension melted away. The kids began to stir in the back seat.

When they reached a pull-out at the top of the mountain pass, Kyle pulled over to let the kids stretch their legs and take in the view. It was beautiful – 62 degrees with a hint of snow at the top.

The boys immediately started throwing snow at each other, laughing in their short sleeves.

As Kyle watched, he heard the rumble of the logging truck passing by. He sighed. Angie gave him a knowing side glance. They both laughed again.

This time, though, Kyle didn't feel the familiar frustration creeping up. It was a freeing feeling.

"See?" Angie said, smiling. "You're already letting it go."

~ ~ ~ ~ ~

I had been looking forward to my high school reunion for years. I know it may sound silly to some, but attending a reunion had been on my goal list since I was in my twenties. And now, here it was!

I was excited to be part of the event's organization and eagerly reached out to the coordinator, offering my experience in event planning and expressing my willingness to help. A few days later, I got a response: I had been assigned to help with decorations.

Decorations?!

I felt a bit flustered, but decided to embrace the role and do it to the best of my ability. A few months passed, and the decoration committee met to discuss how to make everything look perfect for the reunion. I was put in charge of the centerpieces and worked hard to create beautiful, yet affordable, designs. I was proud of what I'd put together and couldn't wait for the event to finally arrive.

When the day of the reunion came, however, there was a hitch. The person who had volunteered to help with cleanup fell ill, and the committee was left scrambling.

I knew I couldn't help – the reunion was scheduled to run until 11 p.m. on a Saturday night, and I had church the following morning.

The leader of the committee was in a panic, trying to find a solution, and as we began the setup, I was approached about helping with teardown. The assumption was that I would be willing to pitch in. And because I hadn't clearly communicated my limitations (I didn't use my words ... aren't we supposed to learn this lesson before kindergarten?), I found myself assigned to cleanup duty.

I was furious. I didn't like this at all. As I set up my centerpieces, my frustration simmered beneath the surface, but I did my best to carry on.

The atmosphere at the reunion was completely outside of my comfort zone: loud music, drinking, and the overwhelming noise of everyone shouting to be heard over the music.

Not only was I struggling with the thought of having to stay for cleanup, but I was also becoming increasingly overstimulated with no real way to escape.

I tried to make the best of it, stepping out of the room a few times to calm my mind, and chatting with the people I knew. But deep down, the tension kept building, and I didn't even realize how upset I had become.

A couple of hours later, as the reunion was winding down, I began to clean up. That's when I noticed people getting irritated by my actions. It didn't help that my own frustration began to show.

My flesh took over, and I found myself getting snippy and impatient. Finally, once the room cleared out, we were able to get everything cleaned up.

What I didn't realize at the time was that I was grunting with frustration as I worked. My good friend, who had stayed to help, later told me that I wasn't very kind. Another friend tried to make casual conversation, and I responded with a snide remark. It was definitely not my best moment.

The next day, I felt deeply convicted. How had I represented Jesus to all those people who didn't know Him? Not well at all.

I allowed my frustration to control me, and in doing so, I failed to reflect His light in that moment. I prayed hard afterward, repenting and reflecting.

I realized that I had gone into the evening with my own preconceived ideas of how things should go, and that was my downfall. I hadn't prepared myself to handle the situation the way Jesus would.

I let my own expectations drive my actions, and that led to a miserable time for me and those around me – far from the memorable time it was meant to be.

It's easy to get in our own way when we think things should unfold a certain way. We set ourselves up for failure when we allow our emotions to take charge.

That's why it's so important to let God be in control. The only way we can do that is to keep our eyes fixed on Him, always expecting Him to work in every situation.

We need to be ready to speak His words, even when our emotions are running high.

Much like Kyle's frustration on the road, my inner battle was a perfect example of how easy it is to let our own flesh take the wheel. He had his mind set on how the drive should go, and when things didn't go as planned – when he was stuck behind that slow-moving truck – his emotions took over. He let his frustration grow, and instead of letting God guide his response, he let his flesh steer him toward irritation and anger. I did the same thing … and was reminded by the Holy Spirit that this is not ok.

The next time I find myself in a similar situation, I know that I need to step back and pray, allowing Him to lead and guide me. It doesn't come naturally, and it's difficult to stay intentional in the heat of the moment, but I know that through Christ, we can overcome our flesh and reflect His light, no matter how we're feeling.

The wise words of Paul assure us that this is possible:

> **Not that I speak [a]from need, for I have learned to be [b]content in whatever circumstances I am.[12] I know how to get along with little, and I also know how to live in prosperity; in any and every circumstance I have learned the secret of being filled and going hungry, both of having abundance and suffering need.[13] I can do all things [c]through Him who strengthens me.**
>
> *–Philippians 4:11–13*

These verses are often taken out of context.

What Paul is saying here is that we can find contentment in all situations through Christ. None of this is possible without Him.

These verses aren't saying that we can do everything. The Greek word translated as "can do all things" is ischyō, and is better translated "to have strength" because this wouldn't translate as well if "can do all things" was inserted.

Verse 13 could read more like this: In every kind of situation, I have strength through Him who strengthens me.

Note: this is my interpretation when looking at the Greek interlinear scripture. The key point here is that Christ is the only way we can move beyond our fleshly impulses and let Him take control.

After all, He's a far better driver. We should simply trust Him to take the wheel.

Chapter 8

It's Starting to Rain

✚

After the kids had played for a while, Angie went to grab the cooler. Kyle sat at the weathered picnic table and it began to wobble. He leaned back, trying to balance on the creaky seat. Angie approached, hefting the cooler toward the table.

Kyle shot up his hands. "I wouldn't do that if I were you!"

But it was too late. Angie slammed the heavy cooler down on the table with a loud thud, rattling the whole thing. Both of them froze, eyes locked, waiting for something to happen. For a tense moment, nothing did. Then, slowly, they both broke into nervous laughter.

"Well," Angie said, "I'm not sure this table can handle the boys."

Kyle grinned. "Oh, I'm sure it can't! Honestly, I'm afraid to move. I think it might collapse. I wonder how long this table has been here?" he asked with a chuckle. He glanced back at the van, then added, "You know what? I'll grab the blanket from the back. Let's have a proper picnic."

With that, he gingerly stood up and headed toward the van.

Meanwhile, Angie got to work making peanut butter and jelly sand-wiches. Kyle laid out the blanket on the scratchy grass, and Angie fol-lowed, carrying the sandwiches.

"Boys! Time to eat!" she called. Despite their intense focus on play, the boys switched gears in an instant, running toward the blanket. Food always had that effect.

Joshua grabbed the first sandwich he could find and held it triumphantly in the air.

"Ha! I win! First sandwich!" he shouted, waving it in front of Jacob, who tried to snatch it from his hands.

"I got it, I got it! You'll never get it!" Joshua crowed.

"Joshua, stop antagonizing your brother," Angie said. "Jacob, come grab another one. There's plenty."

Jacob, confused, turned to his mom. "Ant-ang-inize? What does that mean?"

Angie chuckled. "It's *antagonize*. It means to tease or upset someone on purpose."

Jacob frowned. "He wasn't making me mad. He was making me sad. He's always so mean to me, and that makes me sad... but I guess then I get mad, and that's why I want to punch him."

"Yeah, well," Angie said, sighing, "let's not punch him today, okay? Just eat your lunch."

Joshua, sitting cross-legged on the blanket, poked at his sandwich. "I don't like peanut butter and jelly."

"You liked it yesterday," Kyle said, not looking up from his chips.

"No, I didn't."

"Yes, you did."

"No, I didn't," Joshua insisted, crossing his arms defiantly. "I just didn't want you to know, so I didn't say anything."

Angie sighed, trying to keep her cool. "Joshua, it doesn't matter if you like it or not. It's what we've got. You can eat it or you can go hungry. Your choice."

Joshua glared at her, but after a long beat, took a reluctant bite of the sandwich. Jacob fiddled with his bag of chips, and Kyle leaned over to help him open it, helping himself to a chip in the process.

"Hey!" Jacob exclaimed, eyes wide. "You have your own chips. You don't need mine!"

"Maybe I do!" Kyle shot back with a grin. Jacob rolled his eyes, but dug in.

Suddenly, the air turned cold. The sun disappeared behind thick clouds, and a gust of wind swept through the area. Kyle glanced up, frowning at the darkening sky. Angie, looking up as well, grabbed the edges of the blanket, trying to hold it down as the wind picked up.

"Hurry up and eat!" she urged the boys, "Knees on your plates so they don't blow away!"

The kids scrambled to finish their sandwiches, but before they could even get the last bites in, the rain started. First a few drops, then a torrential downpour. The boys yelled and bolted for the van.

"Mom! The door won't open!" Jacob shouted from the van, pulling frantically on the handle.

Angie jogged over, pulling the stubborn door open with a yank. It often stuck, but she managed to get it.

She turned to see Kyle getting soaked, still scrambling to pack up the cooler. He was too far away for her to reach him, but she jogged over to help anyway.

Kyle was desperately trying to gather up the blanket and trash, but the wind blew it out of his hands. Angie tried to grab the napkins, but they flew away like paper birds.

Frustration bubbled up inside her. "*First, I had to help Kyle when he was stuck behind that stupid truck. Then I had to break up the boys fighting. And now I can't even hold onto the trash!*"

She chased after napkins, plates, and chip bags, feeling like a fool. Meanwhile, Kyle had reached the van, and the boys were laughing and pointing out the window. Kyle followed their gaze, his eyes widening when he saw Angie running in circles trying to catch a chip bag in the wind.

Though the boys and Kyle seemed amused, Angie wasn't laughing. Her irritation was building.

"Why did we even come on this trip? We were fine at home. This was supposed to be a big change for Kyle, but he hasn't considered how this affects the rest of us!"

Finally, she grabbed the last chip bag and stormed over to the trash can, shoving it inside with more force than necessary. She marched back to the van, her soaked hair dripping and her mood even darker.

Kyle glanced at her with a sideways grin, but when he saw her expression, it faltered. The boys fell silent in the backseat.

Kyle gripped the steering wheel, his voice tentative. "Is everything okay, honey?"

"It's fine!" Angie snapped, though her voice was strained. Clearly, it wasn't.

~ ~ ~ ~ ~

Ever had someone rain on your parade? You're cruising along, everything seems to be going right, and then – bam! Someone shows up and drops a bucket of negativity right in your lap. Things go from great to frustrating in an instant.

Not too long ago, I was put in charge of a massive project. I'm talking about a beast with a million moving parts.

Here's just a taste of what I was trying to manage:

1. Volunteer help throughout the project (and the liabilities/protections needed for those volunteers).

2. Material delivery and how that played into installation.

3. Vendor coordination and ensuring that the vendors worked in the right order (not to mention selecting the correct vendors for the job before work started).

4. Coordinating the impacts on ministries and notifying parents and congregants of these impacts.

5. And more!

While I was running around, trying to juggle all of this, this one person kept popping up, pointing out everything that could go wrong. They brought up the negative over and over again. At first, I tried to be patient. But after a while, I got angry. I didn't voice my frustration. Like Angie, I let it fester inside me. I started letting their negativity shape my thoughts. Instead of looking for ways to make it work, I dove into a pit of cynicism.

The timeline was the big issue. Over and over, I was told: "*It's too tight. We'll never make it.*" And you know what? My stubbornness kicked in. I hate being told something can't be done. So I dug my heels in. And you know what? We did. We hit that deadline – barely. I somehow kept the volunteers, the materials, the vendors, and the communication with the church running.

But here's the kicker: I paid a heavy price for it.

Somewhere along the way, I forgot why I was even doing this. What started as a project to create a better space for worship turned into a matter of pride. It became about how I would look if I didn't meet the deadline. It wasn't about the church or the ministry – it was about *me*. And that's where I messed up. My heart got hardened, and I let pride take over.

The truth is, the person who rained on my parade wasn't the problem. They were just pointing out things I needed to hear. The problem was how I responded to the rain. I let my ego control my decisions, and instead of using their criticism to grow, I let it make me bitter. I was more focused on completing the project for my own glory than for God's. And that's dangerous. We are warned against this in Hebrews 3.

Therefore, just as the Holy Spirit says,

"Today if you hear His voice,

[8] Do not harden your hearts as [a]when they provoked Me,

As on the day of trial in the wilderness,

[9] Where your fathers put Me to the test,

And saw My works for forty years.

[10] Therefore I was angry with this generation,

And said, 'They always go astray in their heart,

And they did not know My ways';

[11] As I swore in My anger,

'They certainly shall not enter My rest.'"

– Hebrews 3:7-11

Thankfully, God in His grace helped me to get back on track when I repented of my pridefulness. When our pride gets in the way, we stop allowing God to work.

We will stay in the same place until we allow Him to break our pride. We can think of the tests of the Lord in cycles. It looks kind of like a coil. I'm a visual person, so I've included an image.

In our walk of faith, God will allow us to face tests. These tests are not random but intentional, and they will evolve over time – becoming more complex and challenging as long as we are growing in Him.

Each time we pass a test, we are promoted to the next level of spiritual maturity. But if we fail, we don't move forward; instead, we remain at the same level until we pass. It's like a class – if you fail the course, you have to repeat it.

God allows these tests not to discourage us, but to help us draw closer to Him and grow in holiness.

We can't become more like Christ if we refuse to move forward when faced with difficulty. If we choose to stay stuck in our frustration, bitterness, or sin, we hinder our growth and prevent ourselves from progressing to the next level.

One thing that has helped me tremendously in my walk with Jesus is this: *Expect the test.*

Don't be caught off guard when a challenge arises. Instead of getting frustrated when life throws a "pop quiz" your way, recognize that it's part of the process.

Change your perspective. When you expect the test, your response will change. You'll approach it with more patience, trust, and even joy knowing that it's a chance to grow and deepen your relationship with God.

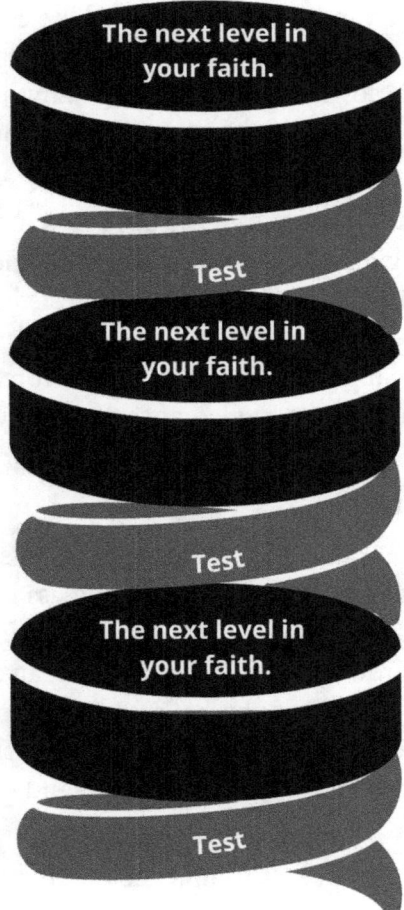

Chapter 9

Drizzle

✟

As Kyle eased the van back onto the road, he could practically feel the tension radiating from Angie. He wanted to help, but he knew better than to try. He'd been down this road before – anything he said might just make things worse. She didn't get angry often, but when she did, it was a storm.

In an unspoken understanding, the boys were unusually quiet in the backseat. Their usual giggles had quieted when Angie shot them the infamous "death glare." They knew better than to test the waters now. Joshua stared out the window, his mind racing. He couldn't help but replay the scene of his mom chasing after the trash, but he forced himself to push the thought away – he almost giggled at the memory.

"Mom would not be happy if I started laughing now. Hold it in, hold it in!" he thought to himself.

Jacob, on the other hand, was fascinated by the steam on the windows. He breathed out slowly, fogging up the glass more, and then began drawing in it with his finger. First, a heart, then an arrow. He added a man and a dog – Andrew and his dog Sparky, on an adventure in the woods. *"Just like me,"* Jacob thought, his mind spinning a little story. The man and his dog were exploring, having fun... until they fell into a hole. *"Oh well,"* he thought, bored with the drawing, and quickly wiped it all away.

"Dad?" Jacob's voice broke through the quiet.

"Yeah?" Kyle's response was tired. The trip was starting to wear him down. Only two more hours to the hotel.

"When are we going to stop? I don't want to be in the car anymore," Jacob whined.

Kyle rolled his eyes internally. *Irony at its finest.* "A couple more hours, buddy. I know, I don't want to be in the car either."

Joshua suddenly gasped from the backseat. "Is there a pool?! I wanna get in the pool!"

Jacob squealed, joining in. "A pool! Me too!"

Angie's voice cut through the excitement like a knife. "Yes, there's a pool. But your dad will take you. I'm staying in the hotel room tonight."

Kyle stole a quick glance at Angie, her body stiff with irritation, but turned his focus back to the boys.

"I'll take you to the pool. But we've still got a couple hours before we get there. How about we watch a movie to pass the time?"

"Yay!" the boys yelled in unison, excitedly settling in.

Kyle fumbled with the controls and got the movie going. He looked over at Angie, still visibly cold and distant. She had that look on her face – the one that said there was more going on than she was letting on. He hesitated for a moment, then decided to speak up.

"Angie, do you want a blanket or something? You look cold."

"I *am* cold!" she replied, her voice laced with exasperation. "But we can't get the blanket. It's all the way in the back, and there's no way I'm getting out now. No pullouts here, and the rain is still coming down in buckets."

Kyle thought for a second, glancing at the road ahead. "Why don't you just unbuckle and grab it? I'll go slow."

"I guess I could do that. It's the only way I'll get some warmth," she said, her frustration easing just a little.

He let off the gas, the van slowing to a near crawl as Angie unbuckled and clambered to the back of the van. She dug through the pile of damp picnic leftovers and retrieved the blanket. It was a little wet from the rain, but not too bad. She wrapped it around herself as she returned to the front seat, settling in with a sigh of relief.

"Better?" Kyle asked, glancing at her with a touch of concern.

"Almost," she replied, but the corner of her mouth twitched in a half-smile. Really, though, it was a yes. She felt much better already. Thanks to Kyle. He almost always knew what to do. Almost.

~ ~ ~ ~ ~

In the previous section, I talked about how we go through tests in life, and in this part, I want to continue that discussion.

In the story, Angie got drenched in the rain, and instead of moving on, she chose to stew in her frustration. It wasn't just about the rain – it was about the way she responded to it. Sometimes, like Angie, we face tests in life, and instead of learning from them and moving forward, we linger in our feelings of frustration or discouragement. We choose to stew.

We need to go through life expecting that God will test our faith. Tests are part of the growth process – whether we're ready for them or not. Think about Angie and how her frustration in the rain was a kind of test. Could she let it go and move forward, or would she let her frustration cloud her judgment and keep her from enjoying the rest of the trip?

Likewise, in our walk with Jesus, we are constantly tested in different ways. Just like in any education or personal development, tests are a necessary part of growth. They reveal what's inside of us and help us become better.

Consider the different tests we face. When we run a race, we are tested physically and mentally. When we go for a job interview, we are tested in our communication and skills. When we are tempted by sin, we are tested in our spiritual strength and resolve.

In Angie's case, her test was not about the rain itself, but about how she would respond to it. Would she hold onto her frustration, or would she recognize that it was an opportunity to trust God, let it go, and move forward?

Testing is everywhere. In life, we constantly administer tests to others or ourselves. When we watch a puppy try to learn a new trick, we're testing its progress. When we analyze a problem at work, we're testing our problem-solving abilities. Even the silver in the ground gets tested to reveal its purity.

Similarly, every test reveals something about us – how we respond under pressure, whether we truly understand what we're facing, and whether we've prepared ourselves in the right ways.

God is all-knowing; He doesn't need to test us to know what's in our hearts. He already knows how we'll respond. But we don't always know what's in our hearts, and we need those tests to help us understand ourselves better. Just like Angie's response to the rain, how we react in difficult moments shows us what we truly need to work on.

I've had moments like this in my own life. For instance, when I was managing that project I, like Angie, let my pride take over. Instead of leaning on God, I started doing things my way.

God allowed me to stay in that place for a while, and through it, I learned how hard it is to do things for Jesus when my heart isn't in the right place. My pride clouded my judgment and hardened my heart, just like Angie's frustration. But when I was ready to let go and turn back to God, He was there, guiding me.

The importance of community became clear during that time. My pride was fueled by a series of negative comments, and I got caught in a negative spiral.

One day, someone said something offhand, "That person is really good at finding problems." And it stuck with me.

It felt like an attack, but over time, God used it to change my perspective. Maybe that person wasn't trying to be critical; maybe they were given the gift of spotting problems so that others could find solutions.

That shift in mindset softened my heart toward that person, as well as more broadly. It was like Kyle offering Angie a blanket.

Sometimes, when we are stuck in our frustration, God sends someone or something to provide the comfort we need to move forward, even if they don't realize the impact they're having.

When you're in the middle of a test, or even after it's over, it's important to reach out to your Christian community. Like Angie, we often want to stew in our frustrations, to be isolated with our thoughts and emotions.

But the enemy loves to isolate us. Just like a lion tries to separate an animal from its herd to attack, the devil tries to separate us from others, using shame, fear, and pride to keep us from sharing our struggles. The devil wants us to feel alone, defeated, and unworthy of grace.

But when we lean into our Christian community, we find strength, support, and encouragement. Together, we stand firm through the tests, and we are able to keep moving forward.

One of the things that makes this especially difficult is how often Christian leaders are isolated. Statistics show that those in leadership are some of the loneliest people in the church, and that loneliness makes them vulnerable to attack.

If you're in a leadership role, or if you know someone who is, don't let that isolation persist. Don't let the weight of expectations separate you from authentic relationships. When people see their leaders as human – just like them – it creates space for honesty and connection.

Lean into the community that God has led you to. If you don't yet have that community, find it. The community God has placed in your life needs you, and you need them.

Like Kyle offering Angie the blanket, sometimes the best way to move forward is to lean on the people with whom God has surrounded you. Don't let preconceived ideas or fear of vulnerability stop you from building those relationships.

Chapter 10

Freezing Rain

As Angie buckled herself back in and began to snuggle into the blanket, the rain suddenly became harder and harder. It quickly turned from droplets to sheets of water, the windshield wipers swishing in a frantic rhythm. The car swerved slightly on the slick mountain road, causing her stomach to flip.

Kyle turned up the wipers, but they couldn't keep up with the rain. Kyle, his eyes focused on the road ahead, gripped the steering wheel with a steady hand.

"We'll be okay," he said, his voice steady, trying to reassure Angie, who was sitting beside him with her hands clenched in her lap.

Angie nodded, trying to convince herself that Kyle was right, but unease settled in her chest. She glanced back at the boys. Their faces were pressed against the windows, watching the storm with wide eyes. Joshua, always the brave one, whispered something to Jacob, who nodded, both of them glued to the spectacle unfolding outside.

Suddenly, the sky got even darker. A sharp crack of thunder split the air. Angie jumped, her heart pounding. The first pellets of freezing rain hit the car like sharp needles, pinging off the metal roof with alarming force. They started small, then became larger and heavier. The sound of the freezing rain pounding on the car was nerve wracking.

Kyle's face was set in concentration as he guided the car around the sharp curves of the mountain pass. Angie's pulse raced, and she felt a wave of panic wash over her. She wanted to trust him – she did trust him – but the storm was so fierce. She knew the road was becoming harder to navigate.

"What if the freezing rain cracks the windshield?" she asked, her voice trembling now. "What if we slide off the road?"

Jacob shuffled nervously in his seat. "Mom, we're gonna be okay, right?"

She forced a smile, but inside, she felt a deep knot of fear.

"Of course we are," she said, her voice weak.

Kyle, sensing her growing panic, spoke calmly, his tone steady and re-assuring. "Ang, just breathe, okay? We'll be out of this soon."

The next few minutes felt like forever. The storm continued to rage around them, but Kyle handled the car with expert precision. Angie sat back, her hands still gripping the seat, but her heart, though still pound-ing, was no longer as heavy.

Once they got about halfway down the mountain, the storm began to ease. The freezing rain subsided and the rain softened, revealing beautiful fields all around them. The road ahead, though still wet, felt less daunting.

Angie closed her eyes for a moment, letting the peace settle within her.

~ ~ ~ ~ ~

We've all encountered that one person who's difficult to work with. They mean well, but they're like a bull in a china shop – clueless about the chaos they're creating. You try to give them the benefit of the doubt, but sometimes, it ends up backfiring.

I had one of those experiences. I let myself become the china in that china shop – and I nearly shattered. But in the end, I came out stronger, despite the potential damage.

For years, I worked hard in ministry and slowly built up my confidence. Growing up in a challenging environment with deep-rooted insecurities, I had faced many obstacles to reach a place where I could stand tall, make decisions, and feel like I was actually doing something worthwhile. It wasn't always easy, but I was getting there. That is, until everything came crashing down.

A new pastor joined our staff, and he had a way of pushing my buttons like no one else could. Looking back, I see now that he was tapping into my insecurities, playing on things I hadn't yet fully dealt with. But I also know that this experience was exactly what I needed to confront those hidden fears and truly step into the freedom I had longed for.

Before this person came along, I had struggled with imposter syndrome. I doubted myself constantly, even though I was performing my job well. Thoughts like *"I don't know what I'm doing,"* or *"If people only knew how unqualified I was, they'd never listen,"* would often creep in. And this new pastor? He didn't help. He knew exactly what strings to pull, and one of those was the accusation that I was controlling.

This was a sensitive issue for me. As the operations pastor, control was part of my role but not in a dictatorial way. I had to know when to take charge, but I also had to know when to step back and let others lead. To be called controlling, though, felt like a direct hit to my confidence. I started to regularly ask myself *Am I being too controlling? Maybe I am just a control freak?*

For about three months, I spiraled. I became consumed by self-doubt, overanalyzing every decision I made and trying to avoid being too controlling, even though it was literally part of my job. I didn't talk to anyone about it I just stewed in my insecurities.

The situation reached its breaking point when this individual was let go. I never had a chance to resolve things with him. I never stood up for myself or confronted my fears head-on. But eventually, I began to open up to the people around me my friends, my mentors, the people who truly knew me. And that's when things started to shift.

What I realized, as I reflected on everything, was that while there were areas where I needed to grow, the bigger problem wasn't me it was what I believed about myself. My insecurities weren't just surface-level; they were deeply embedded in my identity. I hadn't truly embraced the fact that God had brought me to that place for a reason. I didn't fully grasp that my worth wasn't in my performance or in what others thought of me, but in who God says I am.

Even though I wasn't fully secure in my identity at that point, God still reached out and helped me see that He wasn't done with me. My identity wasn't wrapped up in the lies I believed about myself – it was anchored in God's truth about who I am.

Looking back, I'm grateful for the painful process, because through it, I learned that my confidence and identity must come from God, not from what others say or what I fear about myself. We're all going to face challenges and criticisms, and how we respond to those tests shapes who we become. Through this, I learned to step into the freedom of knowing that my worth is secure in Christ.

In the end, even though I nearly shattered, God used the experience to refine me. And I came out stronger, not because of what I believed about myself, but because of what God says about me.

I am not the shame that I was carrying because of my past. Instead:

> **Therefore if anyone is in Christ, this person is a new [g]creation; the old things passed away; behold, new things have come.**
>
> *– 2 Corinthians 5:17*

I am not self-made, but rather:

> **…we are His workmanship, created in Christ Jesus for good works, which God prepared beforehand so that we would walk in them.**
>
> *– Ephesians 2:10*

I am not a lost, insignificant person. I am a child of God:

> **...we are children of God, and it has not appeared as yet what we will be. We know that when He appears, we will be like Him, because we will see Him just as He is.**
>
> *– 1 John 3:2*

My friend, God has brought you to this place for such a time as this.

You are not defined by the struggles or circumstances of today. When you look beyond this moment, to the future He has planned for you, you will understand why He has allowed you to walk through this season.

He is patiently waiting for you to reach out and take His hand, to embrace the identity He has created for you.

The real question is: will you surrender the identity you've built for yourself and step into the true identity you have in Christ?

Chapter 11

Black Ice

✞

The storm had given way to a heavy mist with some soft rain. The moisture clung to the valley full of beautiful golden grass, providing a wonderful shining landscape. After about another 30 miles, the road snaked upward again, and the air grew colder.

Kyle knew something was changing outside. The van started to drive differently. He could feel the tension in the air, like electricity waiting to shock him. He kept his hands steady on the wheel, fearing that the worst was still ahead.

The boys had fallen silent now. They were wiped out from the tension of the storm. Angie, though, had been worried through the whole storm, even more so when the hail started. Her concern had not gone away. Kyle knew she could feel the change in the air too, her silent questioning of whether they should've stayed home, whether it was all worth it. But they were here now. They had to keep going.

The road twisted, and Kyle eased the car into a sharper turn. The tires slid slightly before gripping again. He felt it. He knew how easily things could turn if they lost traction. The road ahead was slick, but not from rain anymore. It was the kind of slickness Kyle knew too well: black ice.

"Is it bad?" Angie asked, concern in her voice.

"Not yet," Kyle replied, but he knew better than to relax. The black ice was worse than rain or snow – it didn't announce itself. It just showed up, suddenly, like a thief in the night, and if you weren't careful, it could take everything from you in a second.

As he rounded another bend, the tires of the car skidded briefly, a jolt that made Angie flinch beside him. Joshua stirred in the backseat, mumbling something incoherent as Jacob clung to him, sensing the tension.

"*I've got it,*" Kyle muttered under his breath. He was talking to himself, more than anyone else. He had to.

His eyes flicked to the road. The ice had formed a thin, nearly invisible layer across the pavement. It was dangerous. It wasn't the kind of ice that looked obvious. The more he tried to concentrate, the harder it became to see the changes in the road. He had to trust his instincts, feel the car respond beneath him.

"Dad," Joshua's voice broke through his focus. "Is it bad?"

Kyle glanced in the rearview mirror. Joshua's face, full of uncertainty, mirrored Angie's earlier concerns. The weight of those questions added another layer of pressure. It wasn't just the ice now; it was the responsibility of keeping his family safe. The weight of *his* responsibility.

"It's fine, buddy," Kyle replied, but even he didn't fully believe it. "Just a little icy. We're good."

But deep down, he knew that "fine" didn't really mean fine. He couldn't let them see how unsure he was, but the cold grip of fear was starting to tighten his chest. It was hard to shake the feeling that things could slip away at any moment.

"*Slow and steady,*" he said to himself.

He eased off the gas pedal, gently applying pressure to the brakes as they came upon another curve. The car slid, just a fraction of an inch, but enough for Kyle's heart to skip a beat. He corrected, keeping his eyes focused on the road. His grip tightened on the wheel, but he didn't panic. He couldn't. He had to stay calm.

"It's going to be fine, but I need to concentrate," Kyle said, his voice growing weaker.

Angie nodded, her face pale but understanding. She didn't say anything – she knew there was nothing more to be said right now. Kyle could almost hear her internal conversation, just like his own. The truth was, no amount of reassurances would make things easier. They both knew that. The mountain and the ice didn't care about reassurances. They cared about whether you were paying attention, whether you trusted the road and yourself enough to get through it.

He eased the car into another turn, the tires gripping just enough for them to stay steady. But this wasn't over. They were still in it.

A few miles ahead, the terrain began to level out, but the danger of black ice remained. There would be no warning before it showed up. Kyle had to read the road. Read the subtle shifts in the air, the sound of the tires on the pavement. As they continued down the road, the tires kept their grip for quite a while. The mist cleared and the sky became a crisp blue. The ice seemed less of a threat, and the road less dangerous. Maybe they were clear of the danger.

Suddenly, he felt the car dip, the tires losing traction again. His body went into automatic mode, making precise adjustments. The ice was there, thin, invisible, but it was there, just waiting for him to make a mistake.

His pulse quickened. "*Almost there,*" he muttered.

They rounded another curve. The worst of the ice seemed to be over, but the road still demanded his full attention. Each curve was a reminder: they weren't out of the woods yet. But Kyle knew that no matter what, he wouldn't give up. Not for himself, and not for his family.

Finally, as the road began to flatten out, the danger of black ice lessened. Kyle let out a breath he hadn't realized he'd been holding. He glanced at Angie, who met his eyes with a tired but grateful smile. She didn't need to say anything. They both knew the worst had passed.

~ ~ ~ ~ ~

I should have seen it coming – the moment when everything seemed to fall apart. Or at least, the moment I thought it was falling apart. I remember the phone call like it was yesterday. It was from my youngest son's school, telling me that he was being suspended for threatening other students.

My heart sank. As I hung up the phone, I shut the door to my office and broke down. I didn't know all the details yet, but I could feel the weight of it. I knew it couldn't be good.

It was a Wednesday, and I was on church staff, and we still had our evening services, including youth group. I made the decision to wait until after youth group to talk to my son. I knew the conversation would be difficult, and I needed some time to process. I had already scheduled a meeting with the school's principal the next morning, and I tried to get through the evening.

I taught my class (thankfully, it was video-based), but my mind was elsewhere. When I finally got home that night, I sat down with my son, and we had the conversation. It wasn't easy, but I was hopeful – after all, we'd been working on better communication for months.

The next morning, the meeting with the principal was one of the hardest I've ever had. I heard accusations I never thought I'd hear. There were concerns about my son possibly having suicidal thoughts. There were so many unanswered questions.

I walked out of that meeting feeling like I had been punched in the gut. Raising our son had never been easy, but this was a whole new level of fear and uncertainty.

I went home immediately after the meeting, my mind racing. In a panic, I gathered up every sharp object I could find, afraid of what I might discover. I took his phone and found evidence of unhealthy friendships and things I never imagined he would be involved in.

My son, the one I thought I knew, seemed like a stranger to me. I was devastated.

It felt like everything was crumbling. But we weren't going to give up. We made the decision to take a break from his friends and media while we tried to figure things out.

Homeschooling became our next step, even though we had no idea how we'd make it work while both working full-time. But we trusted that God was leading us through this storm, even if it didn't feel like it.

That Sunday, when it came time for worship, it was hard to raise my hands. Knowing that God is in control is one thing – but feeling that control is something else entirely. Yet, despite my feelings of fear and uncertainty, I raised my hands anyway. And in that moment, I reminded myself that God was in the middle of our situation, even when it feels like everything is spinning on its head.

Sometimes lifting our hands is easy. Sometimes praise is a sacrifice. The author of Hebrews reminds us to bring that sacrifice to God and choose trust.

Through Him then, let's continually offer up a sacrifice of praise to God, that is, the fruit of lips praising His name.

– Hebrews 13:15

Our emotions can deceive us, but the truth is, nothing surprises God. He knows every detail, every step we need to take. The key is to turn to Him, even when everything feels like it's falling apart. He knows exactly how to pull us out of the tailspin we find ourselves in. And He's waiting for us to trust Him.

Chapter 12

Slipping a Bit

The steady hum of the engine was the only sound in the car as they continued on their trip. Something had shifted in Kyle. The storm had passed, the black ice was behind them, and the road had evened out. But the unease inside him hadn't cleared.

His grip on the steering wheel had loosened, but the tension in his chest was still there, gnawing away. He didn't feel the same sense of relief like he usually did. It had always been his job to keep his family safe, to be the strong one, but now, for the first time in a long time, he couldn't shake the feeling that he had failed them.

He glanced at Angie, her face was pale, and her eyes had become distant. She had trusted him throughout the storm, but he could feel the cracks in that trust, the subtle shift.

"I'll bet she thinks I pushed too hard. She's probably mad that I kept going and didn't pull over."

Kyle's anxious thoughts began to run wild. He couldn't help but consider if his calm demeanor had been a facade. Was he really that calm? Or was he just numb?

The icy road was still fresh in his mind – how close he had come to losing control. How easily things could have gone wrong. That thought looped in his mind, over and over again, like a broken record. If the ice had been just a little more treacherous, if the storm had lasted longer, if his instincts had failed him for even a second – what then?

Kyle's eyes shifted to the rearview mirror. The boys were asleep now, unaware of the quiet tension filling the car. Jacob's head tilted toward Joshua, his little hand resting on his brother's arm as they both slept, innocent and oblivious.

But Kyle wasn't innocent. He wasn't sure if he ever had been. He felt weighed down by the guilt of his irresponsibility.

"What am I trying to prove by taking this trip? Was it always just about me? What about Angie and the boys? I thought it would be a way to honor my dad and get a fresh start in a new place, but maybe I was wrong."

He was feeling suffocated by the weight of the decision. As the car wound through the valley, he continued his downward spiral.

"Maybe this wasn't going to be at all what I thought it would be. Maybe I've been too optimistic. Maybe I've been trying to force something out of this trip."

Kyle wondered if he had been trying to chase down a sense of purpose that hadn't been there in years. After all, he had already been feeling numb and a bit apathetic for the past year or so. When his dad passed away, he knew that he had become despondent. When they went through the will and learned about what his dad had left him, Kyle had felt a renewed sense of vigor. That vigor had covered the numb feeling. Now, he was beginning to slip down the path of discouragement again. He could feel it, but he couldn't stop it.

His mind wandered back to the road, his thoughts growing darker with every curve. What if they had made the wrong choice? What if this trip was just a distraction – a way to cover up the cracks he had been too afraid to repair?

"Am I even still the man Angie married? Or have I lost that person along the way?" he thought, self-doubt hitting him like a cold wave.

For the moment, he felt completely adrift. The mountain had been a test, sure, but it was a test he felt he had failed. It had only shown him how fragile everything really was – the family, the marriage, even himself.

He thought back to their earlier days, when everything had felt easier, clearer. Back when his purpose was so clear. He was young and bright, before responsibilities and routines had dulled the spark. It was always about adventure then, about living – not just surviving.

Now, everything felt so ... mundane. It felt as if he was just going through the motions.

"You okay?" Angie's voice broke through his thoughts, soft and questioning.

Kyle looked at her, startled. She had been watching him, he realized. She always sensed any change in him, recognizing when he began to become depressed almost more than he did. Today was no different. He turned his attention back to the road, suddenly ashamed of how his thoughts had spiraled.

"Yeah. I'm fine," he muttered, though he didn't believe it. Angie didn't either. She had seen this before.

The silence stretched between them, and Kyle fought to push the unease away. He had always been the strong one – the one who had answers, who knew what to do. But now, as he drove through the misty valley, he realized that strength had started to feel like a mask. Maybe he had been holding everything together for so long that he forgot what it felt like to truly feel.

Maybe this trip was a way to prove something to himself, but what if it was a mistake? What if it was all just an illusion of control – a way to chase a fleeting sense of adventure that would never come back?

His mind churned with the questions: *What was he really hoping to find here? Was it peace? Was it purpose? Was it a sense of freedom? Or was it just the quiet desperation to escape?*

"Kyle..." Angie said again, with a slight tremor in her voice. He looked over at her, and the way she said his name made something in his chest tighten.

She was concerned. He could see it in her eyes. Her earlier strength had faded, too. Maybe she felt the same way he did about this trip – the same doubts, the same apathy creeping in.

But he didn't know how to say what was on his mind, how to admit that he was struggling, that everything he thought he knew was starting to unravel. It was easier to keep going, to keep pretending everything was fine, to keep pressing forward with the trip, with the family, with the life he had built. But deep down, he was starting to wonder if any of it was enough … if *he* was enough.

For the first time in a long while, he wasn't sure. And that uncertainty began to gnaw at him.

What was it that he had been chasing all along anyway? It sure wasn't this overwhelming feeling of doubt, of insignificance, creeping into everything he thought he was sure about. Why was everything so wrong?

"Maybe we should head back," Kyle said suddenly, his voice low, almost to himself.

Angie didn't respond at first, but he could feel her eyes on him, searching.

"What do you mean?"

"I don't know… This whole trip…"

His words trailed off, the question he had been too afraid to ask lingering between them. Was this the life he wanted? Was this the life they both needed? Had he been running from something all along – something he was too scared to face?

For the first time in years, Kyle felt small. But he knew that despite this feeling, he must continue on. His family needed him. His legacy needed him. There was light at the end of the tunnel. The question was, how long was the tunnel?

~ ~ ~ ~ ~

Sometimes pressures just pile up. I'm not sure if you have ever experienced it, but there comes a point when you really start to question if it's all worth it. Did God *really* ask me to do this? Maybe I missed what God really wants from me.

I hit this point a few years ago in all areas of my life. It truly felt like everything had come crashing down.

My husband and I had felt the call to begin foster care to adopt a young man. This young man had special needs. We knew that going into it. However, we have two children on the autism spectrum, and one with ADHD as well, so we felt prepared to answer that call. We proceeded with the training and we knew that it was exactly what we were called to do at that time in our lives.

Even as we began the training, my husband and I were asking ourselves some hard questions. Both of us held pretty demanding vocational positions and we knew that this journey to adopt was not going to be an easy one. I mean, did God really ask us to do this?

But time and again we were reminded, yes, He did ask us to do this. We were both so excited about beginning this foster journey. As we drove across the state to meet this young man, we were doing trauma training to learn how to help him through his trauma and heal. The training itself was difficult, especially for me. I had a hard childhood and so many of the things that I had seen in these trainings as I was getting prepared to take him into our home were difficult because they brought up memories about my childhood.

Just like Kyle, I felt so small and weak. It caused me to question. But I believe that these questions are good, they're healthy, and if we're doing exactly what God wants us to do, we come out the other side stronger. In the middle, it can feel like everything is hopeless and falling apart. But afterward, we can see how He knits everything together and begins to make sense of it all.

If you find yourself in a place where you are struggling with anything that makes you start to question and consider veering off of the path that

God has laid out for you, I want to encourage you. God knows your questions. He's big enough to answer them. He's big enough to handle your frustrations and your fears.

Don't allow yourself to believe that He doesn't understand. It's just not true. In our humanity, sometimes it's really easy for us to turn to other people with our frustrations and our fears. Don't do that! Turn to the Lord because He understands all of it more than any other human can. As Paul said:

> Rejoice in the Lord always; again I will say, rejoice! 5 Let your gentle spirit be known to all people. The Lord is near. 6 Do not be anxious about anything, but in everything by prayer and pleading with thanksgiving let your requests be made known to God. 7 And the peace of God, which surpasses all comprehension, will guard your hearts and minds in Christ Jesus.
>
> *– Philippians 4:4-7*

Coming to God with these things is a choice, and it's not an easy one. But I guarantee you that it is much more fruitful than going to your fellow man with all of your frustrations and your questions when you are really wondering what God is doing.

Make no mistake, I'm not negating the value of wise counsel. What I am saying, though, is to not put more faith in wise counsel than you put in God. Trust in Him and what He is doing always.

Chapter 13

Correcting the Swerve

✝

The road ahead seemed to stretch endlessly, the fog rolling thick over the valley like a blanket. Kyle's hands rested loosely on the wheel, his grip wavering as his mind continued to spiral. He should be focused on the road. He knew that.

He should be here, with his family, paying attention to the twists and turns that lay ahead. But instead, his mind kept wandering to the same questions: *What am I doing? Why did I think I could pull this off? What's the point of all this?*

The car hummed steadily along, but Kyle's thoughts were drowning him. The sound of the tires on the wet pavement seemed to fade into a distant hum, swallowed by his self-doubt. Every curve in the road felt like an obstacle, not because of the road itself, but because of the way his mind was racing – paralyzed by insecurities.

He glanced out of the windshield and saw the curve approaching, but he didn't turn the wheel fast enough. The tires hit the edge of the road – gravel instead of asphalt – and the car jolted suddenly, swerving a little too far to the right.

"Whoa, careful!" Angie's voice was sharp, cutting through the fog in his mind. Her hand shot out, gripping the armrest tightly as the car swerved, just missing the guardrail.

The sound of the tires scraping over gravel sent a jolt through Kyle's chest. His heart beat faster, and for a second, his stomach flipped. He quickly corrected the wheel, getting the car back onto the road with a tense breath.

"Goodness, Kyle, are you okay?" Angie asked, her voice strained. She was looking at him now, eyes wide with concern, but there was a tinge of frustration there, too.

"I'm fine," Kyle muttered, his voice barely above a whisper.

His palms felt slick with sweat against the wheel, and he kept his eyes fixed straight ahead, trying to avoid looking at Angie. He wasn't fine. He wasn't fine at all. But he didn't know how to say it.

Angie didn't let it go. "Kyle, what was that? You weren't even paying attention. We almost went off the road!"

"I said I'm fine," Kyle repeated, his voice sharper now.

His irritation flared, not because of her concern, but because of the rising storm in his own chest. He was already struggling to keep his head above water, and now it felt like Angie was only adding to the pressure.

Joshua stirred in the backseat. "What happened? Are we okay?"

"We're fine," Angie quickly reassured him, her voice trying to remain calm for the boys. "We're just fine."

But Joshua's face, pale and wide-eyed, met Angie's in the rearview mirror. He could sense the tension, the unease, even if he didn't fully understand it. He looked at Kyle for reassurance, but Kyle kept his gaze on the road, his thoughts swirling, as if he couldn't get past the weight of his own failure.

"Dad?" Joshua asked tentatively. "Are we okay?"

He had a hard time even asking the question. When he had seen his father like this before, he got really mad when Joshua asked him anything.

Kyle didn't answer right away, his hands still tight on the wheel. He hated that feeling – the feeling that he wasn't enough, that somehow, he was failing his family. His mind kept returning to those dangerous thoughts: *What if I'm not the man they think I am? What if I'm not the father I should be? What if I can't fix this?*

He felt a knot form in his stomach. He hadn't even noticed that he was drifting off the road. He hadn't noticed how little he'd been truly present in the moment. Yet again, another failure.

"Of course we're okay, Joshua," Angie finally said, her voice strained, but her eyes still trained on Kyle. "Dad's just a little tired. It's been a long day."

Kyle's chest tightened. Angie wasn't fooling anyone. Not even herself.

"Stop it, Angie," Kyle snapped, his voice suddenly louder than he intended. He flinched at the harshness of it, but the words were out, and now they hung in the air like an accusation.

"Stop pretending everything is fine. You can't just ... just cover it up and act like this is what we need. Like I can just be fine. I'm not."

Angie's eyes narrowed.

"What on earth is that supposed to mean, Kyle? Of course you're fine. We're still going to make it. You're still in control."

"No," Kyle said, shaking his head, the frustration and self-doubt pouring out of him now. "I'm not in control. I never was. I'm just ... lost, Angie."

His voice broke slightly, but he steadied it, his grip tightening on the wheel.

"I'm trying to keep this family together, trying to make everything feel like it has some purpose, but I don't know what I'm doing anymore. I don't know why I thought I could take us on this trip, why I thought it would fix everything."

He could hear the silence settle in the car, the weight of his words hanging heavy. The boys remained silent, their eyes fixed on him in the rearview mirror, sensing the shift in the air.

Angie didn't respond immediately. She looked at him, her face softening, and for a moment, Kyle felt something like guilt flash through him.

Maybe he was being too harsh. Maybe she was right to push him, to try to keep the peace. But how could she understand? How could she understand how much he was struggling to keep it all together?

The minutes stretched on, and the car felt heavier with every second. He felt Angie's gaze on him, but it wasn't judgmental – just worried, just tired.

Finally, after a long pause, she spoke, her voice quieter now, but firm.

"Kyle... you're right. You don't have all the answers. But that's okay. It's okay to not have it all figured out. But we're in this together, all of us." She glanced at the boys in the backseat. "We're still a team."

She put her hand gently on his arm, hoping the touch would break through his despair.

Kyle swallowed hard, trying to keep the lump in his throat from growing any bigger. He wanted to say something back, something that would make this all feel better, but the words wouldn't come. He could only nod. He didn't know if he believed it, but he knew that Angie believed it, and maybe that was enough for now.

Joshua's small voice broke the silence.

"Are we still going to the new house, Dad?"

Kyle took a deep breath, forcing a smile, though it felt strained.

"Yeah, buddy. We're still going."

Joshua seemed satisfied with that answer. Slowly the tension in the car began to shift, though it was far from gone. There was still the heavy weight of doubt pressing on Kyle's chest, but for the first time in a while, he didn't feel so alone in it.

As they continued down the road, the fog began to lift, the heavy clouds giving way to clearer skies. It wasn't perfect. It wasn't easy. But the road was still open before them, and for the moment, that was enough.

He wasn't sure if he would ever fully feel okay again, but he knew one thing – he didn't have to do it alone.

~ ~ ~ ~ ~

In the last section, I talked a bit about our fostering journey and the call we felt to do it. When we were getting ready to start fostering, I felt weak and small. Even though we knew that fostering was what God wanted us to do, it didn't make the issues that we were dealing with go away. It didn't stop me from feeling weak, but I learned to trust God in a new way despite that weakness. Once my husband and I got past the questions, we felt confident that we could handle what was thrown at us.

Fast forward a few months. We have now met the young man we felt led to foster and got to know him. He began to transition into our home and we started seeing some behaviors, but we knew that those would come. We had prepared ourselves.

Our children, teenagers at the time, had prepared themselves as well. We had many conversations to get ready. Unfortunately, as time went on, fostering became increasingly difficult. My husband and I became more and more stretched. Our children became stressed. Our youngest son began to spiral out of control. Neither of us knew how to help him through it.

Despite the palpable tension that was happening in our family, we continued on. We soldiered through it, knowing that this is what God wanted us to do. But I began to make a fatal mistake. I didn't rely on God as fully as I needed to. I allowed myself to be influenced by my own thoughts and feelings about the situation.

I got distracted and really did begin to feel like I was walking around in a mental fog. I was going through the motions in my day-to-day life. I became an emotional mess. I began to ride a roller coaster of feelings rather than relying on the Rock that is my firm foundation. I began to deal with depression and apathy.

Don't get me wrong, I knew that God was there. But I allowed myself to be sidetracked. As a result of that, I began to fall apart. I remained in this internal strife for some time. I did my best to keep the battle within, but I'm sure it was easy for all who were close to me to know that something was amiss.

Even though it took a while, I did get back on track and began to rely on God again for my strength. At this point though, our family was really struggling. We had begun to spiral, but we were still on the road. We continued to push through even though it was hard.

The behaviors that we were experiencing with our foster son were uncontrollable. And to top it all off, I was being triggered by the behaviors and experiencing new trauma as a result of what had happened in my own past.

I started seeing a therapist and working through some of my trauma. We intensified our family therapy, trying to figure out different ways we could best equip him and our family for success in the placement. We did all we could to keep him in our home. We gave our best effort.

I wish I could say that there was a happy ending to this story. After a few months of living in our home, things had escalated to the point that we knew they could become dangerous for someone. We had to disrupt the placement.

My husband and I were heartbroken. We were both so certain that this is what God had wanted us to do. But it felt like a failure at the time. When you find yourself in the mental spiral of negativity, trying to figure out what exactly you were thinking, you can begin to really spin out of control.

It took me a while to wrap my head around what God was doing. Thankfully, at this point in my life, I had been journeying with God long enough to know that He had a plan, even if I didn't understand it. In hindsight, I can see exactly what His plan was. We were able to impact this young man in such a way that he was able to begin his healing journey, whereas blockades had been put up to stop him from beginning that process previously. He's still a part of our lives, even though sometimes that's a hard thing to balance.

My friend, sometimes life is hard. Sometimes it doesn't make any sense as we go through the motions. I firmly believe that all of us go through these ebbs and flows in our lives for a reason. It helps us to remember who our Foundation is. It reminds us that we cannot rely on only ourselves. It reassures us that God is with us in all situations. And that He cares. And He does care.

> **You whom I have taken from the ends of the earth**
>
> **And called from its remotest parts,**
>
> **And said to you, 'You are My servant,**
>
> **I have chosen you and have not rejected you.**
>
> **10 Do not fear, for I am with you;**
>
> **Do not be afraid, for I am your God.**
>
> **I will strengthen you, I will also help you,**
>
> **I will also uphold you with My righteous right hand.'**
>
> *– Isaiah 41:9-10*

Even though in these verses God is speaking specifically about Israel, He is also saying these words to you and me. Be encouraged by these words that He speaks to our hearts. Let them seep into your soul.

Chapter 14

The Crash

✠

The miles seemed to stretch on in front of Kyle, each one a constant reminder that he was still struggling to find his way. The fact that the road had evened out and fog lifted didn't diffuse the unease inside him. The constant questioning, the fear of inadequacy – it was still there, gnawing at him. He couldn't escape it.

He glanced at Angie, who was looking out the window, lost in her thoughts, her face still pale from earlier. The tension was still there, thick and suffocating, but neither of them knew how to get rid of it.

Kyle kept his hands on the wheel, gripping it just a little too tight, trying to focus on the road, but his mind kept drifting. He was still second-guessing everything.

"What if this whole trip was a mistake? What if we didn't need an adventure, but something simpler?" he thought.

He wasn't sure about anything anymore. But he knew that he needed to keep going. Everyone was relying on him. And they were in this together.

The silence between them felt heavier now. Joshua and Jacob had long since fallen back to sleep in the backseat, their faces pressed against the windows, their breaths soft and even.

Kyle envied their peace, their ability to just be in the moment without the constant weight of doubt.

He shook his head, trying to refocus, trying to push those thoughts aside. But it was hard. His mind raced in circles, his thoughts still racing, when something caught his attention – a flash of movement on the road ahead.

A deer.

A large buck darted out from the trees, its powerful legs propelling it across the road. Kyle's heart leapt into his throat as the animal moved too quickly for him to react, its body almost in the path of the car. He jerked the wheel instinctively, trying to avoid hitting the deer.

His movements were too sudden. Too sharp.

The tires lost traction, and the car began to swerve, first left, then right. Kyle fought to correct, but it was too late. The car was out of control, spinning in a wild, chaotic arc.

The sound of screeching tires filled the air as panic gripped Kyle's chest. He could hear Angie's sharp cry, the sound of the boys waking in the backseat, and then – everything went white.

It all happened so fast.

The van rolled, tumbling end over end, the weight of the moment pulling Kyle deeper into the abyss of fear. His seatbelt dug into his chest, his body slamming against the side of his door with each roll. The world outside was a blur of metal and glass, the sound of the crash deafening.

Finally, the car came to a stop, upside down.

The air was thick with the smell of dust, gasoline, and the lingering scent of rain. Kyle's head was spinning, and his vision was blurred. His heart pounded in his chest, his breathing erratic as he tried to gather himself. His hands still gripped the wheel, though the car was no longer moving.

~ ~ ~ ~ ~

In the midst of the COVID pandemic, I was hired as the operations manager in our church. I knew very clearly that this was the role that God had for me next in my life. I certainly felt overwhelmed by it, but I stepped into it resting assured that God had it. Navigating church leadership during the pandemic was no picnic, but God guided me in it all. He was so good at getting me through every obstacle and over every hurdle I found in front of me.

Another 18 months down the road, the pandemic winding down, I felt the call to transition to pastoral leadership. To be truthful, I didn't know what this might mean, or exactly why. But I knew with certainty it was what God had next for me.

So I pursued it with fervor. My title changed and my duties expanded. What was already a full-time job became even more than that. I wasn't discouraged by this; in fact, I expected it. I knew that with the call comes more – more time, more spiritual guidance, and more involvement. What I wasn't prepared for was the test of reliance.

Over time, I began to slip into a negative thought pattern. I had such a time looking at things positively. All of a sudden I was angry all of the time, frustrated at all sorts of small things, feeling overwhelmed and overworked, and generally struggling with the monster inside. It was a monster that I had allowed to grow. I didn't feel I was doing well at work, and I didn't feel I was doing well at home. Then I crashed. I hit a hard wall. I knew that decisions had to be made, otherwise I was not going to scrape myself off of the ground and do well again.

It was difficult to go through this crisis of identity … this battle with the monster inside. But, if I hadn't I wouldn't be able to show others how to get back up. We all have moments when life gets hard, but the beauty of God is that we are able to move forward through Him.

In **2 Corinthians,** Paul talks about difficulties that we go through in this life. In fact, he had something specific (we don't know what) that was plaguing him. He begged the Lord to take it.

> But he (the Lord) said to me, "My grace is sufficient for you, for my power is made perfect in weakness." Therefore I will boast all the more gladly about my weaknesses, so that Christ's power may rest on me. [10] That is why, for Christ's sake, I delight in weaknesses, in insults, in hardships, in persecutions, in difficulties. For when I am weak, then I am strong.

– 2 Corinthians 2:9-10

Many ministry leaders have had a crash. Simply do a Google search and you'll find them! My mistake was not pressing further into Christ, and pressing more into my own capabilities … which are few! My crash was internal and didn't have any moral failings (other than not relying on God and trusting in myself to do it all). But none-the-less, it was a crash. An internal crash is still a crash. It doesn't matter if people see the crash, it is still valid. And it's still hard.

Despite the fact that my crash was internal, there were numerous consequences for the people around me. Here are a few of them:

- I began to have fractured relationships with my kids and husband.
- My work lost its excellence.
- My home was always messy.
- I was robbed of my joy, and everyone knew it.

It was difficult for me that my crash affected the people around me. I felt like the poison in the environment I found myself in. Even if no one else thought that way, I sure did.

Even more difficult consequences to bear were the ones that no one saw. I regularly felt inadequate. I never had a goal that I was hitting, and I didn't like it at all. I was disappointed in myself. I was emotionally numb and yet emotionally overwhelmed at the same time. I had a hard time focusing, and I couldn't identify any wins … ever.

This is just to name a few of the overwhelming consequences that I experienced. It was very hard to keep going, and I didn't like it one bit.

No one wants to live this way! But let me tell you something wonderful ... something that we say often, but don't always allow to sink into our souls ... God can take us out of the crash. He can pull us out of the rut we find ourselves in. He can change everything, and only He can change everything. We can't rely on ourselves, something we listen to, someone who inspires us, a book that we read, or (fill in the blank).

Here is the other thing: our God is a patient God. He waits for us to make our decision and turn to Him once again. He isn't going to force us to do anything. We have to be willing to rely on Him. We have to choose His way, and not our own. Once we choose to turn to Him again, He begins his work.

In part two of this book, we'll look at how the healing can begin when we decide we aren't going to stay stuck any more.

Part II

Chapter 15

Assessing the Damage

✞

They say that you don't know the true level of your bravery until you find yourself in need of it. As Kyle came to (with a pounding headache, mind you), he realized that he had a choice to make: He could sit and wonder at the situation or he could move.

At first his thoughts were fuzzy, but soon they became as clear as crystal. He was in his upside down van. Angie was passed out in the passenger seat, with a cut above her eye. The boys were both crying in the back, Joshua silently and Jacob not so silently. Kyle could hear them, but he couldn't see them because of the way his seat was wedged. He decided to move.

He couldn't unbuckle his seatbelt. The mechanism wouldn't work.

"*Argh!*" he thought. "*Why won't this stupid thing release!*"

He jiggled and jiggled, yanking as hard as he could. It finally released, and he fell with a thud.

"Kyle?" Angie groaned. "Kyle, where are you?"

"I'm right here!" he cried.

He twisted his body around so he was right up again, but his ankle got caught in the steering wheel. He had to take his shoe off to get it out. But then he was able to right himself and was crouched on the roof of the van.

"Angie!" He stroked her face, but she was not responding. "Angie!" He cried with more urgency. She didn't move. He put his fingers to her jugular vein, and felt a faint pulse. "*Thank you, Lord*!" he thought, relief washing over him.

He looked to the boys. "Boys, Dad's right here! I'm coming to get you out."

Kyle tried to get to them in the car, but couldn't get past the seats that were wedged together when the van rolled.

"*I have to get out*," he thought, looking out his window. It had broken and he could crawl through. He got on his knees and squirmed out of the van. Then he almost fell. He grabbed onto the door with all of his strength and looked around. They were on the edge of a ravine.

"*I don't think I can get the boys out of the van!*" he thought, panic rising in his chest. "*I don't know what to do!*"

Feeling helpless, tears welled up in his eyes. Then he shook his head.

"*NO! It will not end this way. I'm not going down. My family isn't going down. Think, Kyle. Think!*" he thought resolutely.

Suddenly it hit him. His phone had been on the charger in the van. The phone holder attached to the vent, and it held his phone pretty tightly. Maybe he could call for help.

Kyle pulled himself up with some strength that was not his own, and saw that his phone was indeed in the holder. Clambering back in the van, he grabbed the phone.

"Boys, Dad's gonna call for help. It's going to be okay. Are you guys okay? I can't get you out of the van yet, but we will get out soon. I promise."

Joshua nodded. Jacob didn't respond at all, but kept sobbing.

"*I hope that nothing is wrong. He doesn't seem okay.*"

Kyle's thoughts were starting to spin out of control, and he decided to dial 9-1-1 before he went down that rabbit hole.

Kyle fumbled with his phone, his fingers stiff from the cold and the adrenaline still coursing through his veins. He could barely focus on the screen, but he managed to dial the emergency number.

His heart was still pounding, his chest tight with panic, and every second that ticked by felt like an eternity. His mind kept replaying the crash, the roll of the car, the glass breaking, the shudder of metal scraping against the road.

"9-1-1, what's your emergency?" The dispatcher's voice cut through the haze in Kyle's mind. She sounded calm, detached, and for a moment, he wished he could be as composed.

"There's been an accident," Kyle said quickly, his voice unsteady. "We've rolled the car. We're… we're on Route 94. We're hurt, but we're alive. My wife, my two kids … we all need help."

"Stay calm, sir. Help is on the way. Are there any immediate hazards, such as fire or fuel leaks?" the dispatcher asked, her voice reassuring but practical.

Kyle's eyes scanned the scene, the wrecked car still half-tilted on the side of the road. He could see no signs of fire, but the smell of gasoline still lingered in the air.

His gaze darted over to Angie, who was stirring in the van now, clutching her side. Joshua and Jacob both still hung upside down in the van. Jacob was wringing his hands and wailing, his face pale and tear-streaked.

"I don't see fire," Kyle said, swallowing hard. "But there's a gasoline smell. I'm not sure if there's a leak or not."

"Understood. First responders are en route. I need you to stay on the line until help arrives. Does everyone seem okay?"

"We're hurt, but not critically, I don't think," Kyle said, his voice shaky. "I just … I don't know what to do next. My wife can't move well, and my kids … I can't get them out of the car. We're all scared, honestly."

"I understand, sir. You're doing the right thing by staying put," the dispatcher replied, her tone still calm, but now more empathetic. "Help is on the way. Stay with your family, and keep them calm. We'll have paramedics there shortly."

The line went quiet for a moment, but Kyle could still hear the sound of his own breathing, rough and labored.

He looked back at the wrecked car again. It seemed so much more real now, the severity of the crash sinking in. He hadn't really processed the full extent of what had happened until now. The car was mangled, almost unrecognizable. He had almost killed his family. His stomach twisted at the thought.

"*What... what are we supposed to do now?*" Kyle muttered, more to himself than anyone. He was trying to steady his thoughts, to bring some kind of clarity to the chaos.

But before he could think further, the sound of sirens reached his ears. It started as a distant wail, but it grew louder with every second. Kyle's chest tightened even more. He couldn't tell whether the sound was comforting or terrifying.

"You're doing well, sir," said the dispatcher softly. "Help's almost there. Stay calm."

Thirty seconds later, the first police car pulled up. It was a small town police unit, followed closely by an ambulance and a fire truck.

The vehicles came to a halt just behind their wreck, and a few officers jumped out. Kyle felt a sense of relief wash over him – someone else was in charge now. Someone who knew what to do.

"The police just got here," Kyle said into the phone.

"I'm going to terminate the call now, sir," stated the dispatcher. "You're in good hands."

A tall officer with a broad build and a calm demeanor approached Kyle first. He was wearing a reflective vest and carrying a clipboard.

"You the driver?" he asked, his voice steady and firm, but with an undertone of concern.

"Yeah," Kyle responded, his throat dry. "We've been in a rollover. My family … my wife and kids, they're hurt. We need help."

The officer nodded and gave him a quick, assessing look. "I'm Officer Daniels. Let's get you and your family checked out. Stay with me, alright?"

Kyle felt despondent. He watched as paramedics ran over to the van, assessing Angie and the boys. Once they had done initial assessments, the paramedics were able to remove them from the car.

Kyle saw them begin a more thorough check on Angie, taking her pulse and looking at her injuries.

Officer Daniels spoke to Kyle again.

"How are you feeling? Any head injuries? Dizziness? Pain?"

Kyle hesitated. He didn't want to admit how rattled he was, how much his body still ached from the crash. His leg was stiff, and his head was pounding. But it wasn't as bad as Angie's condition.

"I'm okay," he said, though his voice cracked a little. "Just sore. My head hurts, but it's not bad. I'm just … shaken up."

The officer made a note on his clipboard.

"Alright, we'll get you checked out too. You're not the only one to get shaken up by something like this, believe me." His tone softened just a bit, and Kyle saw the understanding in his eyes. "Don't worry, help's here. You and your family are in good hands now."

As Kyle watched the paramedics work with Angie and the boys, tending to her injuries, he felt a strange mix of emotions. Relief, fear, guilt – he wasn't sure how to separate them.

The crash was over, but he could still feel the weight of it pressing on him, threatening to swallow him whole. His thoughts were still clouded with self-doubt, and he wasn't sure when or how it would stop.

But the fact that his family was still here, still together, was something. It had to count for something.

~ ~ ~ ~ ~

When my husband finished college, he was certain that we needed to move back to our hometown. I, on the other hand, was dreading the idea.

While I appreciated the thought of being near family, the painful memories of my past were tied to that town. It was where the people who had abused me lived, where old friendships from my pre-faith life lingered, and where those who knew my troubled history would be there to confront me. The thought of facing that was overwhelming.

Adding to my internal struggle, the church leadership I was serving with didn't want me to leave. They valued my role on staff. They tried to convince me to stay, but deep down, I sensed that there was more to this story – something God was calling me toward, even though I couldn't fully understand it at the time.

A few months before our move, I attended a conference in another state. While the conference itself was impactful, the most significant moment came on the long drive home.

I found myself crying out to God, wrestling with the internal conflict about our move. I pleaded with Him, asking why He was allowing this tension between my husband and I. I even begged Him to prevent the move.

And then, in a moment of clarity, I heard the Holy Spirit speak gently but firmly:

I'm calling you back there. You need to submit to your husband.

It wasn't the answer I wanted, but I knew it was from the Lord. Reluctantly, I surrendered.

A few months later, we moved back to my hometown, and I sank into a deep depression. I felt utterly lost, unsure of my purpose in this new chapter.

After burning out in ministry, I made the decision to stay home and wait on God for what was next – though I had no clear sense of what that would be.

Months passed, and the reality of our finances hit hard. We couldn't make ends meet on one income, so I began applying for jobs. One opportunity particularly excited me, and when I received the job offer, I felt a sense of hope.

But after a year in that role, I felt God calling me to something else. I transitioned to a different position within the same organization, but this new job was far more challenging.

I struggled greatly with my supervisor. She was a kind woman, but something about her – perhaps her tone or the way she communicated – triggered painful memories of my abusive stepfather.

I couldn't quite place what it was, but I knew I was deeply struggling.

One day, while sitting at a stoplight, overwhelmed with emotion, I cried out to God, asking Him to release me from this job. Just then, a song came on the radio that reminded me I needed to wait on His timing, to trust in His plan.

A month later, I could sense in my spirit that is was time to look at jobs. I only applied for one position, and I was thrilled when I received the offer. It was exactly what I needed.

I spent the next three and a half years in that organization, allowing God to heal my heart and prepare me for what He had next.

I had been wounded by my past experiences in full-time ministry, and I needed time to heal and to rebuild a firm foundation in my relationship with Jesus.

During this period, I took the time to deepen my devotional life and strengthen my faith. It was a season of growth and preparation, allowing me to develop the resilience I would need to step back into ministry when the time was right.

When we experience a fall – whether through hardship, disappointment, or failure – we face two choices: we can stay where we are, or we can move forward into what God has for us.

Like Kyle in his crash, we must decide whether to be brave and get back up or to let ourselves fall apart.

Yes, God can be our strength, but only if we allow Him to be. We have to choose to rise, to move forward, and to trust in His call on our lives. The Bible reminds us in the book of Isaiah:

> **Yet those who wait for the Lord**
>
> **Will gain new strength;**
>
> **They will mount up with wings like eagles,**
>
> **They will run and not get tired,**
>
> **They will walk and not become weary.**
>
> *– Isaiah 40:31*

Sometimes what God calls us to feels impossibly big – bigger than we can imagine. But other times His call feels small, even nonsensical, especially if we've already faced a crash.

But in those moments, we must ask ourselves, *Will we choose the path He has set before us? Will we put our hope in Him, even when we don't understand the journey ahead?*

The choice is ours to make.

Chapter 16

Picking Up the Pieces

The paramedics continued to move around the scene, checking the car for any lingering hazards and securing the area. Officer Daniels came over, clipboard in hand, offering a slight nod.

"The van's totaled. We'll need to get it off the road for now."

Kyle's stomach twisted. The van. *It's over,* he thought, feeling the weight of the loss hit him. This wasn't just a broken vehicle – it was a shattered piece of the journey they had started together. The dream of the trip, the freedom of the open road, felt further away now, as though the crash had stolen that future along with the metal frame of the car.

He saw Angie, leaning against the side of the ambulance, still pale but now holding both of their sons close. They were together. They were alive. The wreck was a mess, but the pieces of their family were still intact.

Kyle knelt beside them. Joshua looked up at him, his little face still streaked with tears but showing signs of comfort now that they were being cared for.

"It's okay, Dad," Joshua said softly, his voice full of the quiet wisdom only a child could have after a trauma like this. "We're okay. You'll fix it. You'll fix everything."

He looked at Angie, meeting her eyes, and without speaking, they shared a moment of understanding. There was still so much unknown – the trip, the repairs, the road ahead – but one thing was clear: they would get through this.

"I'll fix it," Kyle said, the words coming out with more conviction than he'd expected.

And for the first time since the crash, his heart began to calm a little. The journey wasn't over, not yet. There were pieces to pick up, both physically and emotionally, but Kyle knew now he could rebuild, just like he always did.

Kyle looked out at the mountains in the distance. There was still a long road ahead, one filled with uncertainty. But now, the idea of moving forward didn't seem impossible.

Although moving forward didn't seem impossible, Kyle felt a surge of overwhelmment when he began to ponder what he needed to do. Angie climbed in the ambulance, talking to the paramedics. The boys were okay. His family was alive. But that didn't make the pain in Kyle's chest go away.

He couldn't bring himself to go back to the family just yet. The guilt was too heavy, the shame too fresh. Every part of him wanted to fix it, to make everything right again, but he couldn't bring himself to ask for help. Not from Angie. Not from the kids. He had failed them, and now he had to fix this alone. That was what a man was supposed to do, right?

"I'll take care of it," he muttered under his breath, though he wasn't sure if he was talking to himself or to the universe. But the words rang hollow in the rain-soaked air, and as he stood there, staring at the empty stretch of road, something in him snapped.

I don't need anyone, he whispered, the self-doubt gnawing at his insides.

Kyle turned away from the scene, ignoring the concerned looks from the paramedics as they finished attending to Angie.

He didn't need anyone to help him. He didn't want to burden them with his failure. Angie had been through enough, the kids too. This was on him.

Kyle climbed into the back of the ambulance, grabbing his bag with all his things – phone, wallet, a couple of jackets – and made his way back to the road. He'd figure it out. He'd fix this.

He barely noticed Angie's voice as she called out to him from behind.

"Kyle," she said softly. "Where are you going?"

Kyle stopped in his tracks but didn't turn around. He wasn't ready for this. Not yet.

"I'm going to handle things," he said, his voice flat. "I need to get the car sorted. I'll be back."

He could feel Angie's eyes on him, but he couldn't bring himself to face her. He was afraid that if he did, he'd see the disappointment. The anger. He didn't want her to see how weak he felt, how lost.

"But Kyle, we need to stick together," Angie said, her voice shaking with concern. "You don't have to do this alone. Please…"

But Kyle just shook his head, not turning around. "I've got it. Don't worry. I'll fix it. I always fix things."

With that, he stepped away, walking toward the road and the uncertainty ahead.

But the longer he walked, the more he realized he was drifting further from the people who needed him the most. He hadn't realized it at first, but now, with each step that he took, the cold sense of isolation began to creep in. He was alone. Alone with his thoughts. Alone with his failure.

He collapsed into the grass, hands gripping his head, tears welling up in his eyes. And then, without warning, the dam broke. The tears came – silent at first, then violent, shaking sobs that wracked his body. Kyle let out a ragged breath, but it didn't help. His chest felt like it was caving in, his thoughts swirling in a dizzying spiral. He wanted to scream, to punch something, but the fear – the overwhelming, suffocating fear – had him trapped in place.

For what felt like an eternity, Kyle sat there, utterly lost in the storm inside his own mind. His thoughts bounced from one thing to the next, every failure, every fear, every doubt. He couldn't make sense of anything.

I'm failing them. I've already failed them.

And that was when the clarity hit – the crushing weight of everything. It wasn't just about the crash, or the car, or the road ahead. It was about him.

Kyle, the provider, the protector, the one who always had everything under control.

And in that moment, he realized just how deeply he had been relying on that image. That image of perfection, of control, was crumbling right in front of him – and it had to.

Kyle didn't need to be perfect. He didn't need to have everything figured out. He was human. He was allowed to break. He was allowed to fail. And, most importantly, he was allowed to ask for help.

The tears didn't stop, but slowly, the storm inside began to calm. It wasn't gone, but Kyle could breathe again. The panic, the anxiety – it had faded, even if just for a moment. He was still shaking, but the weight had lightened, just enough to make room for a sense of reality.

He couldn't fix this on his own. He knew that, but he didn't know how to let go of the pressure to do it himself ... to be strong ... to be the one who held everything together.

But in the silence, he finally admitted to himself, *I can't do this alone.*

~ ~ ~ ~ ~

This is it, I thought. New year, new me. Despite never being one to believe in resolutions, I knew something had to change. I had fallen apart and it was time to find my way back. As a list person, I did what came naturally: I made a list.

1. I'll establish a better work-life balance.

2. I'll spend more time writing.

3. I'll read more.

And so on...

I even broke these down into SMART goals and dove in headfirst, eager to make progress. But there was one problem – or rather, two: I didn't keep God at the center, and I didn't pray over these goals enough.

Looking back now, I'm shaking my head. I knew better. I KNOW better. God should have been at the heart of it all and I should have been praying daily about where He was leading me. But did I? No.

It took me a few months to realize the truth: this wasn't working. Sometimes, God lets us try to figure things out on our own to help us recognize when we need to turn to Him.

I'm a strong-willed person, so I've had to fall flat on my face more times than I can count, just to remind myself that I need to let Him take the lead. And sure enough, I fell hard again in this situation. Within just a few months, my stress was out of control. Our plans are not always His plans.

Don't get me wrong, goals are important, and we absolutely should set them. But goals without God? That's where things fall apart. After stumbling once more, I re-evaluated and dedicated my goals to God. I began to pray earnestly for His direction, trusting Him to guide me where I needed to go.

Watching God work in the pieces of my life, especially after I'd crashed and burned, has been nothing short of amazing. By the end of the year, my life had transformed in ways I never could have imagined. My health was better than it had ever been, my faith was deeper, and I was on the path God had intended for me all along.

I love hiking, and I've found that God often speaks to me through hiking metaphors. On the trail, I do my best to listen closely to what He has to say.

Life, like a hike, is a journey filled with hills and valleys, mountains and gorges, rivers and streams. Sometimes, we're called to climb a steep hill or scale a mountain. Other times, we may just need to leap over a stream or ford a river.

Occasionally, the trail takes a sudden incline, and we know we're in for a tough stretch. Or we round a bend and find ourselves in the thick of a rough patch before we even realize it.

But no matter where the trail leads, it's always headed somewhere, and God holds the map.

Understanding that life's changes, its ebbs and flows, are inevitable helps us to move forward. No season, whether high or low, lasts forever. Remind yourself of that, and surround yourself with people who will remind you, too.

Don't expect yourself to remain on the mountaintop. That's not how it works. And don't believe you'll stay in the valley forever, either. Keep following the trail that God has laid out for you, trust in His lead, and you'll find yourself in a new place.

When the trail gets tough, make your goal smaller and more immediate, but don't move the goal post! When you hit that mark, move toward the next one.

But whatever you do, don't pull a Krystal. Don't create goals without God at the center. Trust me – it's a harder route.

Chapter 17

Out of the Body Shop

Kyle wiped his face with his sleeve, feeling the wetness on his skin. He took a few deep breaths, trying to steady himself. His hands still trembled slightly, but the panic had receded. The worst of it was over.

He broke down, but now he needed to get back to his family. He needed to show them that he was still there, that they were still a family, no matter what happened.

With a shaky exhale, Kyle got up and began to walk back toward the crash site.

Angie looked up when she saw him approach, her face a mixture of relief and concern.

"Are you okay?" she asked softly, her voice gentle but laced with lingering worry.

Kyle swallowed, taking a deep breath. He wasn't sure he was okay, but he was trying.

"I... I wasn't okay for a while," he said, his voice barely above a whisper. He let out another shaky breath and forced himself to meet her eyes. "I'm sorry, Angie. I thought I could fix this on my own. I thought I had to. But I can't ... not without you guys. Not without us."

Angie's expression softened. Without a word, she reached out and took his hand, her grip firm and steady.

"We're in this together, Kyle," she said quietly. "Always have been. Always will be."

Kyle nodded, a small, tight smile pulling at the corners of his lips. The world didn't seem so overwhelming now. They had come this far. They would keep going. Together.

The paramedics had finished their check-ups, and while they still needed a little rest, it was clear that the worst was over. No serious injuries. They would all heal. Physically, at least.

Kyle climbed into the back of the ambulance, settling next to Angie, his hand still in hers. The kids were quieter now, the fear starting to ebb away as they saw their parents together again, no longer divided by the silent storm that had raged between them. The ambulance drove away from the crash site, and headed to the hospital.

And for the first time in what felt like forever, Kyle didn't feel like he had to carry the weight alone. The road ahead was uncertain, but they would face it together. The pieces of their journey, shattered by the crash, were slowly being put back together. It would take time, and the scars would remain, but the most important thing was that they were still a family.

~ ~ ~ ~ ~

When we find ourselves on the other side of a tragedy, when the shock fades and we can finally breathe again, that's when we begin to truly reflect on what matters most.

There's a song that says, "The best things in life are free, but you can give them to the birds and bees. I want money."

I'm here to tell you that the best things in life are not free. They come at a cost. They come with the cost of humility, the cost of trust, the cost of love. These aren't easy choices. Day in and day out, we are given the option to choose these values in our relationship with God and with one another. We can choose to let our hearts grow hard and bitter, or we can choose to open them to the grace and growth God offers.

We can choose to resolve things on our own, apart from God, or we can invite Him into our situations. In the previous section, I talked about involving God in your goals. But we need to go beyond that. God doesn't just want to be a part of your goals – He wants to be deeply involved in every part of your life. He desires an intimate relationship with you, in every moment, in every struggle, in every triumph.

I had a friend once who would imagine Jesus sitting beside her in every situation, and it brought her peace. For me, I find that setting aside time to simply be in awe of God, to reflect on who He is and what He has done – not only in my life but in the lives of everyone – is transformative. It's incredible to think that the same God who created the stars, the universe, and everything in it also cares deeply about me, my struggles, and my relationships.

This is something that we often hear (and even say), but too often, we get swept up in the demands of everyday life, in the noise and the distractions. We don't allow the truth that God is in the everyday seep into our very being.

God's not distant. He's not unconcerned with the details. He cares intimately, and that alone is awe-inspiring. So, I ask you – have you invited God into the details of your life? Have you invited Him into your relationships, your decisions, your difficulties? If not, I encourage you to do so today.

You don't have to carry the weight of your past, your decisions, or your circumstances alone. God wants to walk with you through it all, and He's waiting for you to invite Him in.

Chapter 18

Just a Bump

"Kyle?"

Kyle turned from the waiting room window to see Angie walking toward him, her face still pale but her eyes soft with concern. She had the kids by her side, their little faces full of confusion and a touch of fear. They'd been through so much in such a short time. But Kyle knew he had to focus. This wasn't about him. It was about them.

"We need to call a tow truck," he said, his voice hoarse. "And figure out what we're going to do next. I can't just leave the wreck there."

Angie nodded, her expression unreadable. "I understand, but ... Kyle, let's just take a minute."

But Kyle wasn't listening. His mind was already calculating, already moving forward. They needed a solution, and he needed it now.

He called the tow service. Turned out the police had already told them to bring the wreck to a nearby garage, where they could assess the damage (they were the only place in town, after all). After hanging up, he started looking up nearby rental car agencies. The thought of driving a new vehicle seemed like a weak attempt to right the wrong, but it was the only option left. A temporary fix, at least.

He finally got in touch with someone at a rental agency, explaining the situation and asking if they could get a car to them soon. They were able to arrange something – though it wasn't exactly ideal. It would take a few hours for the car to be delivered to the hospital … and it came with a hefty price tag.

While they waited, Angie helped keep the boys calm. They were hungry, tired, and still a little shaken, but with Angie's steady presence, they found some semblance of comfort. The tension in the air hadn't quite lifted, but it was better.

Once the rental car arrived later that afternoon, Kyle felt a small sense of relief. It wasn't the car they'd planned to use, but it would get them to their next destination. As they loaded what was left of their things into the new vehicle, Kyle could feel the cracks in the road ahead starting to close. This wasn't the end of the trip. This wasn't the end of anything.

It was just a bump. A big one, but it would pass. It had to.

With a deep breath, Kyle slid into the driver's seat. He looked over at Angie and the boys, their eyes bright despite the lingering tension. They were still together. And that, in the end, was what mattered most.

"Ready?" he asked, his voice steady.

Angie smiled softly. "Ready."

And with that, Kyle started the engine, pulling back onto the road. They were on their way again – still uncertain, still working through the aftermath of the crash – but moving forward as a family. And for the first time in a while, Kyle believed that maybe, just maybe, they would make it to the end of this journey together.

~ ~ ~ ~ ~

Here's something I've come to realize: we need each other. Just as it's easy to pull away from God in our hardest moments, it's just as easy to distance ourselves from others when life gets tough. But God created us for relationship – He designed us to depend on one another, to learn, grow, and walk through life together. Unfortunately, when we face struggles, our natural instinct is often to isolate ourselves, thinking we need to carry the weight alone.

I remember a time when my children were young, and my husband was serving in the military. During that season, I was blessed with some deeply meaningful friendships. These relationships became a lifeline for me, and we spent so much time together – day in and day out. It was early in my journey with Jesus, and I had just begun to open up about building real, vulnerable relationships.

Before that, I had plenty of surface-level friendships, but this was something entirely different. I decided that as I followed Jesus, I would allow myself to be authentic with others. These friendships were my first true, deep connections in my walk with Christ. There were four of us, and we were inseparable … until I was betrayed.

Throughout my life, I've had moments of overwhelming sadness – times when the weight of life felt unbearable. During those moments, I would often turn to a friend or my husband for support to help process my emotions. One day, in the midst of such a dark time, I reached out to a friend to talk. Afterward, another person from our group called me and shared something heartbreaking. The friend I had just confided in had called me a "downer" and told others how much of a burden I was.

At that point, I was already struggling with deep depression. The weight of those words crushed me. I was grateful to the friend who had the courage to tell me the truth, but the betrayal still stung deeply. It was a gut-wrenching moment, and in that moment, I faced a choice: I could shut everyone out – build walls around my heart to protect myself – or I could confront the pain, forgive, and continue nurturing the relationships that truly mattered.

I chose the latter. I knew that putting up walls would only isolate me more and make healing that much harder. So instead of retreating, I leaned into the friendships that were healthy, trusted the two friends who had remained by my side, and confronted the hurt directly. I decided not to walk this journey alone.

The friend who had betrayed me, though we still spoke, was no longer a close confidant. She gradually drifted away from our close-knit circle, and eventually, our paths separated. But the bond I had with the others only grew stronger. I learned that, even in the face of pain, deep, genuine relationships are worth fighting for. We need each other – not just in the good times, but especially in the difficult ones. And even when we're hurt, choosing to lean into love and trust again is always worth it.

In those moments of hurt, I needed those friends. I needed people who could remind me of who I was in Christ and point me to Him as my source of strength. They shared their own stories of God's faithfulness to help me remember that He is more than enough, especially in my moments of discouragement.

We all need friends. We all need wise counsel to help carry our burdens and support our growth. Because, in the end, we're not meant to walk this journey alone. We can find this several places in Scripture.

As iron sharpens iron,

so one person sharpens another.

Proverbs 27:17

[9] Two are better than one because they have a good return for their labor; [10] for if either of them falls, the one will lift up his companion. But woe to the one who falls when there is not another to lift him up!

Ecclesiastes 4:9-10

So if you find yourself struggling with friendships, I encourage you to reach out. Find someone who can be close to you. Be vulnerable, even though it's hard. Choose trust. God will do powerful things in and through your relationships if you let Him.

Chapter 19

Driving Once Again

✟

The rental car hummed steadily along the road, the engine's soft purr a reminder that they were, at last, back on the move. The air still carried the fresh scent of wet earth and pine. It felt like a new beginning, as though the road ahead – despite everything – held something more than just miles to be crossed.

Kyle was so conscious of the weight of the wheel in his hands. As he drove, he felt a different kind of strength in himself, one that came from having made it through the worst and still moving forward.

He had failed. Yes. But that failure hadn't broken him. It hadn't broken them. They were still together, still a family. And that was enough to keep him going.

Angie sat beside him, her hand resting on his leg, a small but steady comfort as she gazed out the window at the passing landscape.

Joshua and Jacob were both in the backseat, their heads resting against the windows as they dozed, worn out from the day's events. Kyle stole a glance at them in the rearview mirror, his heart swelling with a renewed sense of responsibility – not just to protect them, but to show them that resilience wasn't about never breaking; it was about how you got back up when you did.

"We're getting closer," Angie said, breaking the silence. She sounded calm, but there was an excitement in her voice that was contagious.

Kyle nodded, eyes on the road ahead. "Yeah. Just a few more hours, and we'll be there."

They were heading toward the homestead. The place that Kyle's father had left him in his will, tucked away in the quiet hills of the country. It had been Kyle's dream, too, growing up – his escape, his place of peace. This house and the stories his father had talked about had always seemed so far away, an idealized memory of a simpler time, but now it felt like something more. It was their next step ... a place to breathe, to heal, to begin again.

As the sun sank lower in the sky, casting a soft golden hue over the mountains, Kyle couldn't help but think about his dad. It had been over a year since his father passed away, but the homestead, now his to take care of, felt like the last piece of him left behind. He hadn't been sure about coming here – after the crash, after everything – but now that they were on the road again, he was ready. It was time to honor his father's memory, to create new memories there with Angie and the kids.

He could feel the change inside him as he drove. He no longer felt like he was fighting against the weight of failure; he was starting to accept that the bumps in the road were part of the journey. He didn't have to control everything. He didn't have to be perfect. The road wasn't about getting to some idealized destination – it was about moving forward, step by step, no matter how rough the terrain.

The landscape began to change as they neared the homestead. The once dense forests opened up to wide, rolling meadows with tall grass swaying gently in the breeze. The view of the valley below them was breathtaking.

The air was cleaner, fresher, the weight of the world feeling a little lighter as they descended into the valley. Kyle could already see the outline of the old farmhouse, nestled at the base of a large hill, surrounded by fields that stretched on for miles. His father had always spoken about how this place felt like home, like the land was part of him.

As they turned onto the gravel road leading up to the homestead, a sense of peace settled over Kyle. This was where he could finally let go of the past and start fresh. He had been so caught up in trying to fix everything, to be everything for his family that he had forgotten what mattered most – the simple things. The moments shared together. The act of being present. And the land itself – quiet, grounding, constant.

"We're here," Angie said, her voice soft, as though sensing the shift in Kyle's mood.

Kyle parked the car by the front porch of the house, his eyes drinking in the familiar view – the old wooden barn, the overgrown garden, the vegetable patch his dad had once been so proud of. He couldn't help but smile as he stepped out of the car. It felt like home, even though so much had changed.

The car came to a stop and the kids jumped out of the car, running toward the house. They were eager, full of energy and excitement, unburdened by the weight of the journey that had been so heavy on Kyle's mind. They ran toward the front steps of the house, their laughter carrying through the air. For a brief moment, Kyle allowed himself to relax, watching them. They were alright. They had made it. And now they were here – together.

Angie joined him on the porch, standing by his side as they watched the boys explore the old yard.

"I can't believe we're finally here," she said, her voice filled with awe.

"I know," Kyle replied, taking a deep breath. The air smelled of earth and grass, of life and renewal. "It's ... it's good to be here."

They stood there for a while, simply watching the world around them. The sun dipped lower, casting long shadows across the fields, but the warmth of the evening sun felt different now, as if the storm of the last few days had washed away the weight of their worries.

As Kyle glanced at Angie, he knew this was just the beginning. There would be more challenges ahead, more difficult moments, but the foundation they were starting to build here – on this land, with each other –

would be what carried them through.

The homestead wasn't just a physical place. It was a new chapter, a chance to rebuild and redefine who they were, not as a family of survivors, but as a family that had learned to live and love beyond their struggles.

"Let's go inside," Kyle said, his voice steady but warm. "It's time to make this place our own."

Angie smiled and nodded, and together they walked into the house, ready to create something beautiful, something lasting, in this place they would now call home.

It wasn't just a piece of land left to him by his father anymore – it was a fresh start, a chance to let go of the past and move forward, as a family. It was their future, their new road to travel, and it was wide open before them.

~ ~ ~ ~ ~

No matter how you look at it, none of us want to face the break-down. In fact, we often go to great lengths to avoid it altogether. But sometimes, the breakdown is exactly what we need. We don't have to go searching for it, but we can lean into God during the rebuilding.

Our God is a builder – after all, Jesus was a carpenter. While you're not just a piece of furniture, you are a masterpiece that He is carefully de-signing.

Let that sink in: you are a masterpiece in the making. But if you don't allow yourself to be shaped and molded, like sanding wood into its final form, you'll end up as a wobbly chair – unstable and incomplete.

You need to ask yourself some important questions. Are you going to stay stuck where you are, or will you allow God to take you to the next level He has prepared for you? Will you continue to strive in your own strength, or will you lean into the infinite strength of the Lord to carry you through?

²⁸ Do you not know? Have you not heard?

The Everlasting God, the Lord, the Creator of the ends of the earth

Does not become weary or tired.

His understanding is unsearchable.

²⁹ He gives strength to the weary,

And to the one who lacks might He increases power.

³⁰ Though youths grow weary and tired,

And vigorous young men stumble badly,

³¹ Yet those who [a]wait for the Lord

Will gain new strength;

They will [b]mount up with wings like eagles,

They will run and not get tired,

They will walk and not become weary.

Isaiah 40:28-31

This strength comes from Him and Him alone. He is the one who sustains us, lifting us to new heights we could never reach on our own. Don't try to do it by yourself. Let Him be your strength – every day, every minute, every hour. Lean on Him fully.

In John 16:33, Jesus makes it clear that difficult times are inevitable. You might not be facing hardship right now, but rest assured, challenges will come. When they do, will you allow God to break you down so He can rebuild you stronger than before?

My encouragement to you is this: let God be the one to do the building. It's one thing to acknowledge that we need God to do what only He can do, but it's another thing entirely to allow that truth to penetrate our hearts and souls.

The only way He can shape us into the masterpiece He's designed is if we allow that truth to sink in – and often, it's in the midst of hardship that we truly learn to rely on Him.

Yes, tribulations will come, but remember, they are nothing compared to the incredible plans God has prepared for you.

> **For I consider that the sufferings of this present time are not worth comparing with the glory that is to be revealed to us.**
>
> *– Romans 8:18*

So, will you let Him? Will you allow Him to build you up? Will you surrender to what He has, knowing that it is infinitely better than you can imagine?

Chapter 20

Where You Belong

✝

As they stepped into the old farmhouse, the children squealed with joy. Kyle paused in the doorway, taking a deep, steadying breath. The scent of oil from the worn wooden floors mingled with the faint tang of dust in the air, stirring something deep within him. This was home. He felt it in his very bones.

Kyle glanced at Angie, and their eyes met. She felt it too.

The journey here had been arduous, but it wasn't as though life before the journey had been much easier. Life always came with its share of challenges. But now, as they stood on the threshold of a new chapter, Kyle knew that everything was about to change. Here, in this old farmhouse, his family would find not just a home but a renewed sense of purpose and connection.

"Go pick out your rooms!" Angie called to the boys, her voice light with excitement.

Joshua and Jacob didn't need to be told twice—they bolted up the creaky staircase, their laughter echoing through the house. Kyle stood for a moment longer, still marveling at his fortune. This place, this dream he'd all but given up on, was his. And it wasn't just the house—it came furnished, a treasure trove of memories waiting to be rediscovered.

The trials of the journey hadn't lessened the wonder of this moment. If anything, they had deepened it. Maybe those struggles had been necessary, he mused, a crucible to remind him of the beauty of what he now had. Maybe they had helped him realize just how much his family meant to him.

Kyle shook his head, smiling at his wandering thoughts. He turned to Angie, his grin widening. "Let's check out our room," he said.

Hand in hand, they strolled down the hallway, their footsteps soft on the aged floorboards. The walls were lined with old photographs, each one a portal to the past. Kyle stopped in front of a picture of himself as a boy, dressed as a clown. "Look at that," he said, chuckling. "Me at five. That red face paint stained my skin for days. Mom was so mad!"

Angie laughed. "You were adorable, though," she teased.

Further down the hall, Angie stopped abruptly, her gaze fixed on another photo. "Oh, look at this one!" she exclaimed.

It was a wedding portrait of Kyle's grandparents, their faces alight with joy. Kyle studied it, marveling at how young and happy they seemed. "I only met them once," he murmured. "Can you imagine living in their time? What a different world that must have been."

Angie nodded. "I can't even fathom it," she said softly.

At the end of the hall, they reached their bedroom. Kyle pushed the door open to reveal a space that felt as though it had been waiting just for them. Sunlight streamed through the lace curtains, casting patterns on the walls. Everything about it was warm, welcoming, and perfect.

Kyle turned to Angie, his heart full. They had made it. After all the struggles, all the uncertainty, they had arrived. Now, in this house filled with history and hope, they could plant their roots. Together, they would build a life as solid and enduring as the farmhouse itself.

~ ~ ~ ~ ~

In the last chapter, I mentioned that sometimes things have to fall apart for God to put them back together. Let's delve a bit more into this, and how it can take a great difficulty to allow Jesus to build us up. Even though the crash is hard, even though it hurts, even though it is terrifying … sometimes that is when God shows up and makes a huge change in our minds, in our lives, and in our families.

To be clear, I am not saying that a moral failure or breakdown is what we need to find that anointing. I'm talking about allowing God to use a systematic, physical, or even an emotional breakdown.

The beauty about God is that He knows what we need, and if it even needs occur. It would be wonderful if we never had to go through this, but I believe that we have to allow God to use these breakdowns should they occur. We do a disservice to Him if we don't.

Kyle's journey in the mountains and the challenges he faced along the way, are not unlike the path we each walk when we step into the calling God has on our lives.

Just like Kyle, who was navigating unfamiliar terrain, each of us will face moments where the road feels uncertain, where our confidence wavers, and where we question whether we're truly equipped for the journey ahead.

But walking in our anointing – our God-given purpose – is about trusting in God's guidance, even when everything seems to be falling apart.

The Uncertainty of the Path

In the beginning, Kyle was distracted, second-guessing his decisions, and overwhelmed by self-doubt. He didn't know if he was the right person for the job, if he had the strength to keep going, or if he was even making the right choices. But God had already given him everything he needed to succeed – just like He's given each of us everything we need to walk in our anointing.

When we face difficulty, it's easy to pull away from God. We can become so consumed with the fear of failure or the weight of responsibility

121

that we forget that the Holy Spirit is with us, empowering us for the journey. But we have to remember that God has already equipped us. Our anointing isn't based on our own abilities – it's a gift from God that empowers us to do what we can't do on our own.

As Kyle faced the storm, the ice, and the accident, he found himself grappling with fear and a loss of direction. Yet, even in those dark moments, he could have chosen to step forward with faith – trusting God not just with the destination but with the journey itself.

Walking in your anointing is about choosing to move forward even when the path is unclear. It's stepping out in faith, knowing that the God who called you is with you every step of the way.

Our faith is tested in the hardest moments, and those are the times when God's anointing becomes most evident in our lives. It's in the difficulty, the pain, and the unknown that God does His most powerful work.

When Kyle tried to handle everything on his own after the crash, he was struggling to control a situation that was far beyond his ability. It wasn't until he recognized the need to rely on others, and ultimately on God, that he could begin to move forward again.

The anointing is not about self-reliance – it's about surrendering to God and trusting that He will equip us with what we need. Just as Kyle needed his family, friends, and even the strangers who helped them, we need God and His community to walk in our anointing.

Then, as Kyle finally made his way toward the homestead his father had left him, he began to see the journey in a new light. He started to understand that the purpose of the trip wasn't just about the destination but about the lessons learned, the growth, and the strength that came from overcoming the obstacles along the way.

In the same way, walking in your anointing is not just about reaching a final goal – it's about the transformation that happens in the process.

The anointing God has placed on your life is something that grows with you. It's through the setbacks, the pain, and the triumphs that we learn to rely on Him more, trust Him more, and reflect His power more clearly.

Just like Kyle's journey was about more than just getting to his father's homestead, your journey in walking in your anointing is about growing in faith and allowing God to shape you into the person He's always intended for you to be.

In the end, Kyle found his way, and so will you. Just as Kyle's journey, with all its struggles and triumphs, led him to a place of healing and purpose, so too will your anointing guide you through the highs and lows of life.

The key is to trust, to move forward in faith, and to rely on God's strength, knowing that He has already equipped you for the journey ahead.

Walking in your anointing is about surrendering to God's plan, knowing that He will provide everything you need, and trusting that the path, though sometimes difficult, is leading you to something far greater than you can imagine.

Chapter 21

Planning for the Trip

That evening, as Kyle stood on the porch, watching the evening light soften over the rolling hills, he found himself lost in thought. The warmth of the sunset was soothing, but a quiet tug in his chest reminded him of the weight he still carried.

The journey to this place, to the homestead that had once felt like a distant dream, had been anything but smooth. It hadn't been the adventure he had imagined, the perfect escape he had hoped for.

He thought back to the days leading up to the trip – how he had meticulously planned every detail, thinking that if he could just control everything, if he could ensure that every moment went according to plan, everything would be fine. But nothing had gone according to plan.

The crash, the panic, the doubts – none of it had been part of the equation he had worked so hard to perfect.

Kyle's grip tightened slightly around the railing of the porch, his eyes tracing the fields before him. It wasn't just the accident. It was how he had been mentally and emotionally unprepared for what was to come.

He had assumed that simply arriving at the homestead would be the end of the journey. That once they were here, everything would feel right.

But now, standing on this land, Kyle realized that his preparations had been all about the external – routes, gas stations, food stops, schedules – and nothing about the internal. He hadn't prepared his heart for the journey.

His thoughts drifted back to the moment after the crash – that moment of total helplessness, when everything had spiraled beyond his control. He thought he could manage it all – he thought he was strong enough to shoulder it alone.

But the truth was, he wasn't. The strength was never in holding everything together by sheer force of will. It was in letting go. Letting himself be vulnerable.

He could have prepared better. Not by studying maps or making sure the car was in perfect condition, but by preparing his heart to be flexible, to trust that life – and the journey – would not be perfect and that was okay.

As the breeze lifted the strands of hair off his forehead, Kyle opened his eyes and looked at Angie, standing just a few feet away, her hand resting on the back of one of the rocking chairs. She was watching him, her gaze soft, but there was understanding there, too.

She had been waiting for him to catch up, to realize that no one expected him to do it alone. She had never asked for perfection from him – only for his presence, his honesty.

He realized, too, that this was what the trip was really about. Not the place, not the destination, but the people he was with and how they navigated the chaos together.

The car crash had been a catalyst, but it wasn't the end of the story. It was just a part of the story, a chapter that would make the rest of it that much more meaningful.

He wasn't here just because of his father's legacy. He was here because this was where he and his family would build something new – together.

Kyle sighed, the weight of his realization slowly lifting as he turned to Angie, his heart feeling a little lighter. He didn't have all the answers. He might never have them. But he could start by being more present, by listening, and by letting go of the need to fix everything. The road would always be uncertain. But with Angie and the kids, he realized that was the beauty of it.

Kyle exhaled, his chest feeling lighter than it had in days. The road ahead was still uncertain, but he was ready – ready to embrace the messiness, the imperfections, and most of all, the journey itself. This was their path together. And that was more than enough.

He looked toward the house again, the homestead now standing tall in the twilight, waiting for them to step into it.

This wasn't the trip he had imagined, but it was the trip he needed. And, more importantly, it was the trip they needed as a family.

~ ~ ~ ~ ~

Preparing your heart for ministry is a deeply personal and spiritual journey. It's not just about acquiring skills – it's about deepening your faith, cultivating humility, and aligning your heart with God's purpose.

The foundation of ministry lies in a strong relationship with God. Before serving others, invest in prayer, Scripture, and worship.

Jesus reminds us in **John 15:5**:

> *I am the vine, you are the branches; the one who remains in Me, and I in him bears much fruit, for apart from Me you can do nothing.*

Your effectiveness in ministry flows directly from your connection to Him.

Check your motives. Are you in ministry to glorify God or for personal recognition?

Galatians 1:10 challenges us:

> *10 For am I now seeking the favor of people, or of God? Or am I striving to please people? If I were still trying to please*

people, I would not be a bond-servant of Christ.

Honest self-reflection keeps you grounded in serving for His glory.

Compassion is essential. Ministry is about walking alongside others in their struggles and joys.

Romans 12:15 encourages:

> *Rejoice with those who rejoice, and weep with those who weep.*

A compassionate heart allows you to connect meaningfully with people, sharing in their victories and offering comfort in their pain.

Authenticity is vital. Be real about your struggles and victories, as **2 Corinthians 12:9** reminds us:

> *⁹And He has said to me, "My grace is sufficient for you, for power is perfected in weakness." Most gladly, therefore, I will rather boast about my weaknesses, so that the power of Christ may dwell in me.*

When you're honest about your journey, you build trust and inspire others by showing God's grace in your life.

Ministry requires obedience to God's leading. **Proverbs 3:5-6** teaches:

> *Trust in the Lord with all your heart and do not lean on your own understanding. ⁶In all your ways acknowledge Him, and He will make your paths straight.*

It's not about your agenda but faithfully carrying out God's purpose.

Excellence in ministry honors God. **Colossians 3:23-24** reminds us:

> *²³Whatever you do, do your work [a]heartily, as for the Lord and not for people, 24 knowing that it is from the Lord that you will receive the reward [b]of the inheritance. It is the Lord Christ whom you serve.*

Serve with dedication and skill, knowing you reflect God's character through your work. We will all make mistakes, and perfection is impossible. However, if we aim for perfection, we can attain excellence in our character and ministry.

Ministry is demanding, so care for yourself. **Mark 6:31** shows Jesus telling His disciples:

> *[31] And He *said to them, "Come away by yourselves to a secluded place and rest a little while."*

To pour into others, you must refill your own cup through rest, prayer, and self-care.

Challenges will come, but perseverance is key. **James 1:2-4** urges,:

> *[2] Consider it all joy, my brothers and sisters, when you encounter various]trials, [3] knowing that the testing of your faith produces endurance. [4] And let endurance have its perfect result, so that you may be perfect and complete, lacking in nothing.*

Trust that God uses even hardships for your growth. Even when it doesn't feel good, persevering through the difficulties grows us and prepares us for what God has next.

Above all, rely on the Holy Spirit. **Acts 1:8** promises:

> *[8] but you will receive power when the Holy Spirit has come upon you; and you shall be My witnesses both in Jerusalem and in all Judea, and Samaria, and as far as the remotest part of the earth.*

Ministry is not about your strength but the Spirit working through you.

Ministry is a long-term calling. Stay focused on the ultimate goal: glorifying God and serving others.

Preparing your heart for ministry is ongoing. It's not about perfection – it's about faithfulness.

Let God shape your heart, and trust Him to equip you to serve with humility, love, and authenticity. **Philippians 1:6** reassures:

> *[6]For I am confident of this very thing, that He who began a good work [a]among you will complete it [b]by the day of Christ Jesus.*

Epilogue

How to Know You're on the Right Road

✝

A year had passed since they arrived at the homestead. The land had become a quiet witness to the transformation of Kyle and his family. They had worked the fields, fixed the barn, planted a garden where his father's vegetables had once thrived.

Slowly but surely, the house had begun to feel like theirs – not just in ownership, but in the deep, steady rhythm of living there, together.

Kyle sat on the front porch one afternoon, a mug of coffee warming his hands as he watched Angie and the boys working together in the garden. Joshua and Jacob were laughing, their faces streaked with dirt, while Angie tended to the rows of vegetables they'd planted just a few months before. They were growing. Not just the plants, but the family itself.

As he sat there, listening to the sounds of his family working and playing, Kyle reflected on the journey.

It wasn't just the road that had changed him – it was the choice he had made to keep going, even when things had seemed impossible. When everything had felt broken, when doubt and fear had nearly taken over, he had made the choice to trust – to trust in Angie, to trust in the boys, and most importantly, to trust in himself.

In the days after the crash, Kyle had wondered if he had made a mistake. If the trip, the dream of the homestead, was all just a foolish attempt to run away from the complexities of life.

But now, sitting on the porch, watching his family laugh and work together, he knew.

He had made the right choice.

The trip had been harder than he ever imagined. The accident, the moments of self-doubt, the feeling of being completely unprepared for what was to come – those had all been part of the process.

He realized that life wasn't about avoiding mistakes or controlling every detail – it wasn't about being perfect, about knowing exactly what to do or when to do it. It was about the moments in between – the moments when they had come together as a family and leaned on each other.

Kyle remembered his father's words – how he used to say that life wasn't about finding a destination, but about becoming the person you were meant to be along the way.

His father had lived on this land, quietly, with strength and simplicity. Now, Kyle was learning that lesson in his own way. He had learned to face his fears, let go of his burdens, and open himself up to the people who loved him most.

He smiled as he watched Joshua and Jacob run toward the house, their laughter carrying in the air, and Angie standing beside the garden, wiping her brow.

The stress of the accident, the crash, the doubts – all of that had faded into the background. What remained was a sense of peace – a sense of purpose.

~ ~ ~ ~ ~

Kyle's Journey: A Mirror of Faith

Kyle's journey wasn't just a treacherous drive through icy mountains – it was a spiritual and emotional battle, a raw reflection of the heart-wrenching yet transformative path of following God. It's the kind of journey where fear, doubt, and uncertainty threaten to break you. But in the breaking, God refines you, strengthens you, and draws you closer to His heart.

At his breaking point, Kyle questioned if it was worth the struggle. But conviction, not comfort, kept him moving – a fierce love for his family compelled him forward.

Following God often means choosing purpose over ease. **Luke 9:23** calls us to take up our cross daily, moving forward even when the road feels unbearable.

Through fear and self-doubt, Kyle was transformed. The chaos didn't just challenge him – it changed him. He became braver, stronger, and more rooted in his faith.

Trials refine us like fire purifies gold. **James 1:3-4** teaches that perseverance leads to maturity, shaping us into who God created us to be.

After the crash, Kyle thought it was over, but doors opened in unexpected ways. What seemed like failure was God's hand at work. Trust in God aligns circumstances beyond our understanding. **Proverbs 3:5-6** urges us to trust Him, knowing He'll make our paths straight.

The real gift wasn't a smooth road, but the presence of Kyle's family and the growing faith that carried them together.

In our walk with God, it's His presence that sustains us. **Psalm 23:4** declares:

> *Even though I walk through the valley of the shadow of death, I fear no evil, for You are with me; Your rod and Your staff, they comfort me.*

Kyle's path was riddled with doubt, fear, and failure, but it was also filled with growth, trust, and transformation. Following God doesn't mean a perfect life – it means trusting Him through every step.

In the end, it's not about knowing the destination – it's about trusting the One who walks beside you. Hebrews 12:1-2 urges us to run the race with perseverance, fixing our eyes on Jesus, the author and perfector of our faith. Like Kyle, let your journey refine you and draw you closer to the heart of God.

Author's Note

Hey traveler, you've reached the last page – but the journey of faith never really ends.

Walking with Christ is like a road trip, full of twists, turns, and unexpected detours. My hope is that this book has been a roadmap to help you stay on course and keep moving forward.

But don't stop here! If you're looking for more discipleship resources, visit drivenfaith.org for devotionals, videos, and tools to fuel your journey. I love hearing from readers, so please drop me an email at drivenfaith24@gmail.com.

Also, let's get this message out to more travelers!

Snap a picture or take a video with your book, post it, and tag Driven Devos on Facebook, Instagram, YouTube, or TikTok.

Let's flood the roadways with the gospel!

And if this book has blessed you, please take a moment to leave a review. Your words can help others decide to take this journey, too.

Thanks for riding along with me. Keep your hands on the wheel, your eyes on Christ, and let's keep driving faith forward.

Acknowledgments

First and foremost, I give all glory and honor to my Lord and Savior, Jesus Christ. Without Him, this book would not exist, and without His grace, I would have no story to tell. Every word is a reflection of His faithfulness, and it is my deepest prayer that this book points hearts back to Him.

To my husband, Joe, you are my greatest earthly blessing. Thank you for walking this road with me, encouraging me when I doubted, and loving me as Christ loves the Church. Your steadfast support and belief in me have been a reflection of God's love in my life.

To my family and friends: your prayers, encouragement, and love have carried me through this journey. Thank you for being the hands and feet of Jesus in my life, reminding me to stay the course even when the road felt uncertain.

To my church family and mentors: thank you for your wisdom, guidance, and spiritual covering. Your discipleship and example has shaped my faith, and I am forever grateful for the ways you have poured into my life.

To my readers: this book is for you. Whether you are on the mountain or in the valley, I pray these pages remind you that God is writing your story and that He is with you in every twist and turn. May you find hope, truth, and encouragement within these words, and may your heart be drawn ever closer to Him.

Finally, to the One who is the Author and Perfecter of our faith – thank You for this journey, for the trials that refined me, for the grace that sustains me, and for the privilege of telling Your story. May all of this be for Your glory alone.

With a grateful heart,

Krystal

About the Author

Krystal Hammer is an operations pastor, business owner, and advocate for personal growth and healing. She designs and implements systems that drive efficiency, creating environments where ministries and individuals can thrive.

Krystal is passionate about relationship-building as a powerful tool for developing people, guiding them toward a common goal, and inspiring them to discover their purpose.

A central aspect of Krystal's passion is to help individuals heal from trauma and process their experiences in a supportive, compassionate environment. She recognizes the importance of emotional and spiritual healing in overcoming adversity and works tirelessly to create pathways for people to not only heal but also find hope and restoration.

As a mother of three, including two on the autism spectrum, Krystal also is passionate about advocating for those who think differently, ensuring they have the resources and support to succeed.

Whether through personal mentorship, discipleship, or a community of care, Krystal aims to provide tools and support for individuals to move forward with strength and resilience.

In addition to her professional and family life, Krystal shares devotional content through Driven Devos, using her platform to share wisdom on leadership, faith, healing, and personal development.

She enjoys reading, writing, gardening, and hiking, and cherishes time with her family playing video games and creating lasting memories together.

Coming Soon!

Christian Study

☐ Miles of Faith Study Guide

☐ Unshackled: Healing from Trauma with Truth

☐ Bound by the Darkness: A Battle for Redemption Across Time

Children's Book

☐ Every Skunk has a Purpose

Also by Krystal

Christian Study

☐ Life in Christ: Lessons from James

☐ Driven Faith Devos: Devotions to Make a Difference in Your Life